Emma Ewing

Cooking and castle-building

Emma Ewing

Cooking and castle-building

ISBN/EAN: 9783744785938

Printed in Europe, USA, Canada, Australia, Japan

Cover: Foto ©Lupo / pixelio.de

More available books at **www.hansebooks.com**

Cooking and Castle-Building.

BY

EMMA P. EWING.

BOSTON:
JAMES R. OSGOOD AND COMPANY.
1880.

PREFACE AND DEDICATION.

To GRACE GREENWOOD:

MY DEAR FRIEND,— To you who so nearly fill my ideal of a true American woman, I would like to inscribe this little volume; but as it is more especially written for younger women than you and I, the proper thing, I presume, is to ask you to permit me to dedicate it to your artlessly charming daughter.

I know right well you will cheerfully grant the request. But before doing so, I fancy you quizzically inquiring, and myself gravely informing you, about the nature of the volume, somewhat in this wise:—

"Is the book a novel?"
"A little like a novel."
"Or, is it a cook-book?"
"A good deal like a cook-book?"
"Or, a volume of sermons?"
"Very like a volume of sermons."
"Ah, well! then it must be a good book."
"O yes! a remarkably good book."

Therefore, in the hope that she will find pleasure in its perusal,

"COOKING AND CASTLE-BUILDING"

IS

Dedicated

TO ANNIE LIPPINCOTT.

No woman of her age, I am very confident, can read it without profit. And no housewife, I flatter myself, can carefully follow its directions and advice without doing something to aid on the cause so dear to your and my heart, by having her table supplied with well-prepared food; and thus helping to secure for herself, her family, and her friends, that most desirable of earthly attainments— A PLEASANT HOME.

CONTENTS.

CHAPTER I.

HOW IT HAPPENED.

In New York. — Plans and Projects Ventilated. — Cooks and Cook-books Discussed. — Where shall we Spend the Summer? — The Question Settled. — Off to Maplewood, . . 9

CHAPTER II.

HOW WE MADE BREAD.

Alice Makes Yeast. — The Way She Made it. — About Yeast. — Setting the Ferment. — Preparing the Sponge. — Working the Dough. — Letting it Rise. — Miss Beecher on Bread. — Making the Loaves. — Baking Bread. — French Twist. — Care of Bread, ... 16

CHAPTER III.

STILL DABBLING IN DOUGH.

Graham Bread. — Rolls. — Egg Rolls. — Bread without Potato. — When to Set Ferment. — Soda Denounced. — Cream Biscuit. — Strawberry Shortcake. — Maryland Biscuit. — Alice as Cook. — Her First Breakfast. — What She Prepared, and How She Prepared it, ... 31

CHAPTER IV.

FOOD AND FANCY.

Fried Chicken. — Graham Gems. — English Muffins. — Graham Cakes. — Mushes. — Directions for Cooking them. — Oatmeal. — Crushed and Cracked Wheat. — Hominy or Grits. — Stewed Chicken. — Stewed Meats. — Alice's Adventure. — Alice's Dream. — Gerald Douglas, ... 49

CHAPTER V.

GRIDDLE-CAKES AND OTHER THINGS.

At Breakfast. — Chat about Cakes, Griddles, and Greasers. — Bread Cakes. — Waffles. — Flannel Cakes. — Muffins. — Buckwheat Cakes. — Corn Bread. — Dodgers. — Muffins. — Slappers. — Something about Ghosts, ... 66

CHAPTER VI.

BREAKFAST-TABLE GOSSIP.

Coffee. — How to Roast Coffee. — How to Make Coffee. — A Bachelor's Letter. — English Breakfast Tea. — Black and Green Teas. — Mandarin Tea. — How to Make Toast. — Fanny's Letter. — Pease. — Asparagus. — Green Beans. — Dried Beans. — Pork and Beans. — Stewed Corn. — Corn Oysters. — About Potatoes, ... 83

CHAPTER VII.

AT DINNER.

A Dissertation on Soup. — About Roasting Meats. — Searing Meats. — Dry Roasting. — How to Sear and Roast Meat. — Boiled Meats and Fowls. — Salt Meats. — To Boil Ham. — Beets, Onions, Cabbage, and other Vegetables. — Suitability of Food. — Things that Eat Well Together. — Rice Pudding. — Butter. — Boiled Rice. — Steamed Rice. — A Visit to Mrs. Douglas's Rooms. — Susannah's Story. — Family Portraits. — Mysteries, ... 104

CHAPTER VIII.

OMELET AND DAINTY DISHES.

Chicken. — Beefsteak. — Lamb Chops. — Mutton Chops. — Broiling without a Gridiron. — How to Broil. — Broiled Quail. — Canvas-back Ducks. — Terrapin. — Mrs. Rose's Omelet. — Her Trials and Failures. — Her Final Success. — How the Omelet was Made. — Chicken Salad. — Salad Dressing. — Frizzled Beef. — Mrs. Douglas's Letter. — Emeline Annoyed, ... 123

CONTENTS. 7

CHAPTER IX.

IN THE ORCHARD.

Moralizing. — The Prince of Fruits. — Cooked Apples. — Sugar and Spice. — The Flavor of Fruits. — Canned Fruits. — Fruit Mushes. — Jams and Jellies. — Apple Pie. — Cousin Kate v. Parson Beecher. — Cambric Tea. — Linen Pie. — Baked Apples. — Stewed Apples. — Tapioca Pudding. — Fruit at Meals. — Sugaring Berries. — On the Veranda. — Gerald's Musings, ... 140

CHAPTER X.

EDIBLES AND EDUCATION.

Egg-Plant.— Fried Squash.— Fried Oysters.— Scalloped Oysters. — Fish-Balls. — Hashes. — Scrapple. — A Stew. — Personal Matters. — Cousin Kate's School Project. — Boarding-Houses. — Homes. — The Professor's Story. — Beds and Blankets. — House-work. — Drudgery. — "A Shy" at Reformers. — The Reform Most Needed. — Proper Home-Training of Girls, ... 165

CHAPTER XI.

LITTLE THINGS.

About Cake.— Bread Cake.— Buns. — Doughnuts. — Pickled Cabbage.— Tomato Sauce.— Cucumber Catsup.— Cucumber Pickle. — Spiced Peaches. — Spiced Damsons. — On the Veranda after Tea. — An Interchange of Thoughts. — Cousin Kate on Little Things. — Good-by to Maplewood, . . 190

COOKING AND CASTLE-BUILDING.

CHAPTER I.

HOW IT HAPPENED.

My cousin Emeline, after a two years' sojourn in Europe with her only child, Alice, had returned, and was loitering in New York, undecided as to where they should spend the summer.

Abroad, Alice had devoted herself assiduously to French, German, and music, while her mother had employed much of her time in writing a novel.

One day in early June, a fortnight after their arrival in the American metropolis, Emeline, looking up from the book she had been reading, exclaimed,—

"'O for a lodge in some vast wilderness!' Another week of this horrible din and confusion will be the death of me. Day and night it is one unceasing uproar. Kate, where can we hide ourselves for three months and enjoy uninterrupted rest, while I revise that book of mine?"

I answered her by asking, "Would you mind going to Westfield?"

"I feel just now as if I would not mind going to the ends of the earth, if necessary, in search of undisturbed quiet. But why go to Westfield?"

"Because my friend Jennie Douglas has a beautiful place there, which has been shut up for a year, and will so remain for a year longer. The place is left in care of the gardener; but I have leave to go there when I will, and stay as long as I see fit,—why not bury ourselves there? We might bribe the gardener and his wife to keep our presence a secret as much as possible."

"The very thing," responded Emeline. "Let us start to-morrow. But where shall we get our rations while there, and who will cook them for us? If we install a retinue of servants in the house, we may as well abandon all thought of rest or comfort."

"I have a plan," I said, after a moment's reflection, "which will help me carry out a pet project of my own, and at the same time enable us to dispense with servants."

"My adorable Kate! proceed, divulge, explain. I am all eagerness to know what pet project of yours can be subserved by our burying ourselves for three months in some out of the way place. I fail to see how that will do away with the evils of intemperance, or give the suffrage to woman."

"Emeline, in my wandering to and fro upon the earth, I have been in a great many houses, and have eaten of the labors of a great many cooks. But the houses that deserved to be called homes, wherein genuine comfort and cheerful happiness dwelt peacefully together,— I could count them all on my ten fingers. In searching for the cause of this great lack, I cannot attribute it entirely to the tyranny of man, or the servitude of woman. I am forced to the conclusion that women fail to appreciate the importance of the Home. That in their just rebellion against lives of drudgery and toil, they fail to see how much of this drudgery is self-imposed, and what a grand work each woman might do in her circumscribed sphere if she could make the home attractive and desirable above other places, to husband, sons, and brothers. I have an idea that if the women who are wives and mothers would bring all their powers to bear in the right direction — making it their first object to see that the home is comfortable and attractive,— a place where the husband can rest, and the sons find pleasure,— that these wives and mothers would constitute the most effective temperance crusaders; that the labors of the women who go forth to pray with and convert the rumseller, would, in comparison with their labors, count as nothing."

"Kate, I protest against being forced to listen to your lecture on moral reform. Come to the point. What is your pet project?"

"Why, this: you see, Cousin Emeline, no home can be what it ought to be, unless there is a good cook in the establishment. A great many of the sins of the world are traceable to bad food. A carnal stomach has often more to do with crime than a carnal heart. A popular writer says, 'you may make houses enchantingly beautiful, hang them with pictures, have them clean, airy, and convenient; but if the stomach is fed with sour bread and burnt meats, it will raise such rebellion that the eyes will see no beauty anywhere.' Indeed, I cannot conceive of a man being a Christian husband or father who is fed regularly upon half-baked bread, burnt or raw beef, and vile tea and coffee. Comfort with most of us is essential to happiness. And I have seen the peace of a whole family destroyed for the day by having muddy coffee for breakfast. Now, Emeline, I'm coming to the point. For years this matter has been a burden upon my mind, day and night. I have been longing to reach the ears and hearts of my countrywomen upon this subject. At last the longing has taking shape and form, and I see now in what way I can approach them. As so much of wealth and happiness, as well as enjoyment, is dependent upon the food we eat, and as no home can deserve the name without a well-ordered table, I have concluded to write a cook-book."

"Write a cook-book! Well, why in the name

of all that is sensible, didn't you say so? But I can't for the life of me see how your writing a cook-book will remedy the evils of which you complain, or enable us to dispense with servants at Westfield. We have a perfect library of cook-books already, and of making them there appears to be no end. It requires an ordinary lifetime, almost, to even glance at the thousands and tens of thousands of recipes our numberless cook-books contain, many of them proved perfect, and handed down from generation to generation, along with the family china and silver. Don't do it, Kate."

"Cousin Emeline, you fail to comprehend my purpose. I'm not going to add another to the list of abominations miscalled cook-books, in which it is impossible to find a recipe whereby an unskilled or inexperienced housewife can make a loaf of bread equal to that made by our best bakers. In this one, which I pick up at random, I find only eleven recipes in any way touching bread,— not one of them minute and careful in detail,— while I find in it sixty for cake, and fifty-eight for pies and puddings. From glancing over our popular cook-books, one would be apt to conclude the leading prayer of their writers was, 'Give us this day our daily pastry.' In *my* cook-book I will deal with the essential articles of food. I will dilate upon the charms of bread, meats, and vegetables, at their best; and omit those non-essential, and indigestible messes and mixtures, that have been heretofore thrust so prominently forward. Cook-book makers seem to take it for granted that everybody knows how to make bread, broil a steak, cook a potato, etc., etc. Yet these are the very things that are almost universally spoiled, and rendered unfit to eat, by the average housekeeper. There are plenty of women—ten to one I might say truthfully—who can make nice cake,—but can't bake good bread, or broil a beefsteak or mutton-chop properly. It is said: 'A fair Charlotte-Russe is easier to gain than a good cup of coffee; and you shall find a sparkling jelly to to your dessert where you sighed in vain for so simple a luxury as a well-cooked potato.' In this retreat of ours, we will have undisturbed sway in the kitchen as well as in the parlor, and I will do the cooking in order to illustrate the perfection of my recipes and methods."

"And a sorry time we will have, I fear, in eating the results of your experiments," retorted Emeline; "but no matter; anything is preferable to this horrid New York life. Let us call Alice, and see if she consents to our plan."

Alice not only consented, but was greatly delighted at the prospect of this novel summer in the country; and still more that she would have an opportunity of penetrating the mysteries of the kitchen, or, as she expressed it, of "dabbling in dough."

So the question was speedily settled. And armed and equipped with chintz wrappers, linen aprons, and rubber gloves, we arrived in due season at Maplewood, where, in the grand old kitchen, Alice and I were to be found, morning and evening, with rare exceptions, all through that delightful summer, learning our lessons in the science of cookery.

CHAPTER II.

HOW WE MADE BREAD.

I was indulgent to Alice, and for three days allowed her to wander at will about the grounds and through the maple forest near by,— to sit upon the verandas, where clambering roses and sweet honeysuckle scattered perfume on every breeze that stole into the house,— to drink in the song of birds until her heart overflowed with music. Then, one morning, interrupting her in a trill, which, for low, sweet melody, rivalled the robin's song, I said quietly,—

"Alice, my child, come to the kitchen and make the yeast, for to-morrow we bake."

Stifling a half sigh, Alice ran after me, whirling and dancing as she went; and this is the way she made the yeast:

She put her small hand into the bag of hops, and brought it out full of the dried blossoms. These she placed in a tin stew-pan, and pouring upon them a quart of boiling water, left them to boil five minutes, while she stirred to a smooth paste a gill of flour with a little cold water. Then, through a tin strainer, she poured the boiling hop-water slowly upon the paste, stirring continuously that it might grow thin by degrees, and perfectly mix with the hop-infusion. She boiled this thin starch for a few minutes, stirring it while on the range, lest it should settle and burn on the bottom of the pan. Then she returned it to the bowl, adding a large spoonful of salt and the same of white sugar. When this mixture had cooled to blood heat — or say 98° Fahrenheit — she added a gill of yeast procured from the baker. Stirring all well together, she covered the bowl closely, throwing over it several folds of blanket to protect it from draughts of air, and left it to ferment or rise. Five or six hours later, finding it getting light, she gave it a good beating, which caused it to settle; and this she repeated several times during the day, until the yeast was "quiet" enough to be poured into a glass jar, covered, and set away in the cellar.

Each week during the summer this process of making yeast should be repeated, always reserving a gill of the old yeast to start the new, and always washing and scalding the glass jar with care. If at any time your old yeast should be unfit to start the new with, and you are unable to procure any of a baker, yeast cakes will answer the purpose.

It is less trouble to make yeast and keep it on hand, than to send to the baker's for it when required; besides, yeast made in this manner is superior to that used by most bakers. In winter it will keep two weeks. Glass is better than stone for keeping yeast, being less porous, more easily handled, and more readily cleansed.

At nine o'clock in the evening we set the ferment for the next day's baking. Into a large earthen bowl we put four medium-sized potatoes, — pared, boiled, and mashed, the same as for the table. The water in which they boiled, we drained carefully away. Many cooks use this potato-water to set the ferment; but "the potato, nutritious and harmless as it appears, belongs to a family suspected of very dangerous traits. It is a family connection of the deadly nightshade, and other ill-reputed gentry, and sometimes shows strange proclivities to evil, — now breaking out uproariously, as in the noted potato-rot, and now more covertly in various evil affections. For this reason, scientific directors bid us beware of the water in which potatoes are boiled — into which it appears the evil principle is drawn off; and they caution us not to shred them into stews without previously suffering the slices to lie for an hour or so in salt and water."

To the potato we added a pint of flour, and, gradually, two quarts of boiling water, stirring the mixture constantly meanwhile. When all the water was in, the contents of the bowl resembled thin starch. When the temperature of the ferment had cooled to blood-heat, we added a gill of our new yeast, stirred it well, and covered it closely, that it might retain its warmth unchilled till morning.

Upon entering the kitchen next morning, I found Alice already there.

"Have you looked at the ferment?" I asked.

"No, Cousin Kate, I dare not touch anything in your absence, lest I do mischief; but, pray, let me see it. Why, it looks like sea-foam. How very lovely!"

"Yes," I replied, "and were you to taste it, you would find it not unpleasant, but a little sweet and biting to the tongue. And now, from this pan of flour, which we first sift and warm, we will add to the ferment a handful at a time, stirring and beating it well meanwhile, until it is thick as batter; then covering, leave it to rise. When light again, and fairly dancing with life (or is it the dance of death?), give it more flour and a good beating. This whipping seems to take all the life out of the batter, but you will find that the dough quickly recovers its old spirits, and is all the lighter for the heavy strokes given it. You will observe, Alice, that I put no salt in the bread, there being enough in the yeast to prevent it from tasting fresh or flat. No one, I think, can like to taste salt in bread."

"Cousin Kate, why do you set the ferment to rise in an earthen bowl instead of a tin pan or wooden tray?"

"Tin does not protect the ferment from cold air as does this thick earthenware; and wooden vessels are clumsy to handle, and difficult to keep clean and sweet. Bear in mind, Alice, that you cannot have perfect success in bread-making, if you allow the ferment or sponge to change temperature, alternating from cold to heat; you must not permit it to take a chill, and then force it into a fever by means of hot-air baths. Such treatment will utterly demoralize any bread-sponge. Start the bread at blood-heat, then keep it well covered; and whenever you add flour, let it be of a moderately warm temperature.

"When the sponge is too stiff to be stirred and beaten in this manner, put your hand into it, and work it very thoroughly, adding flour slowly until the dough clings together and seems to have a decided character of its own. The sides of the bowl will then be clean of dough, and you can lift the mass all together, and place it on the bread-board, where you will knead it for half an hour longer, adding flour only as is necessary to keep the dough from sticking to the board or hands.

"When it works clean on the board, and seems lively and spirited, it is well moulded; but test its temper in this way: give the dough a deep poke with your fist, and if it takes the insult meekly and settles down on the board, it is not worked sufficiently; but if, on the contrary, it seems to resent the assault, and springs back after your retreating hand, it is all right.

"Instead of kneading a large mass of dough on the moulding-board, it is better to divide it, working the several parts alternately. Not only because it is easier to mould in small parcels, but because fermentation during the interval of rest softens and renders it lighter than if continuously moulded.

"We will divide this dough into two parts, one of which we will place in this earthen bowl, which has been warmed and well greased, you perceive, and, covering closely, set aside to make into French twist after it has again risen. The remaining half we will subdivide into four parts, making each into a round mass; then by rolling it back and forth under the hand, bring it into a form resembling these bread-pans, which are four or five inches wide, eight or ten long, and six deep; and made, you observe, of sheet-iron, not tin. But for the weight, I would prefer to have them of cast-iron.

"Having warmed and greased the pans, put the loaves in, and set them on the table close together, covering them first with a towel, then with several folds of woollen blanket or other cloth, reaching to the table on all sides, thus excluding the air from the pans. Bread covered in this way rises evenly, and never has a dried, stiff surface before it is baked.

"This bread will need to stand in the pans to rise about an hour, perhaps longer, the exact time required depending upon the quantity of flour added at the last kneading, the temperature of the bread when put in the pans, the state of the atmosphere of the room, the size of the loaves, and other circumstances. To decide when bread is just light enough is a very nice point, and not less important than difficult; for, if you put it to bake a moment too soon, you fail to realize all the good which your labor has entitled you to; while, if you permit it to pass the point of perfect lightness, you lose the best results of your toil.

"Here, Alice, read what Miss Beecher says upon the subject of bread, in the 'American Woman's Home.'"

"The true housewife makes her bread the sovereign of her kitchen — its behests must be attended to in all critical points and moments, no matter what else be postponed. She who attends to her bread only when she has done this, and arranged that, and performed the other, very often finds that the forces of nature will not wait for her. The snowy mass perfectly mixed, kneaded with care and strength, rises in its beautiful perfection till the moment comes for fixing the air-cells by baking. A few moments now, and the acetous fermentation will begin, and the whole result be spoiled. Many bread-makers pass in utter carelessness over this sacred and mysterious boundary. Their oven has cake in it, or they are skimming jelly, or attending to some other of the so-called higher branches of cookery, while the bread is quickly passing into the acetous stage. At last, when they are ready to attend to it, they find that it has been going its own way; it is so sour that the pungent smell is plainly perceptible. Now, the saleratus-bottle is hauled down and a quantity of the dissolved alkali is mixed with the paste, — an expedient sometimes making itself too manifest by greenish streaks and small acrid spots in the bread. As the result, we have a beautiful article spoiled, — bread without sweetness, if not absolutely sour.

"In the view of many, lightness is the only property required in this article. The delicate, refined sweetness, which exists in carefully kneaded bread, baked just before it passes to the extreme point of fermentation, is something of which they have no conception; and thus they will even regard this process of spoiling the paste by acetous fermentation, and then rectifying that acid by effervescence with an alkali, as something positively meritorious. How else can they relish baker's loaves, such as some produce, drugged with ammonia and other disagreeable things; light, indeed, — so light that they seem to have neither weight nor substance, but with no more sweetness than so much cotton wool?

"Some persons prepare bread for the oven by simply mixing it in the mass, without kneading, pouring it into pans, and suffering it to rise there. The air-cells in bread thus prepared are coarse and uneven; the bread is as inferior in delicacy and nicety to that which is well kneaded, as a raw servant to a perfectly educated and refined lady. The process of kneading seems to impart an evenness to the minute air-cells, a firmness of texture, and a tenderness and pliability to the whole substance, that can be gained in no other way.

"The divine principle of beauty has its reign over bread as well as over all other things; it has its laws of æsthetics; and the bread which is so prepared that it can be formed into separate and well-proportioned loaves, each one carefully worked and moulded, will develop the most beautiful results.

"After being moulded, the loaves should stand usually not over ten minutes, — just long enough to allow the fermentation going on in them to expand each little air-cell to the point at which it stood before it was worked down, and then they should be immediately put into the oven.

"Many a good thing, however, is spoiled in the oven. One thing should be borne in mind as a principle: that the excellence of bread in all its varieties — plain or sweetened — depends on the perfection of its air-cells, whether produced by yeast, egg, or effervescence; that one of the objects of baking is to fix these air-cells; and that the quicker this can be done through the whole mass, the better will the result be. When cake or bread is made heavy by baking too quickly, it is because the immediate formation of the top crust hinders the exhaling of the moisture in the centre, and prevents the air-cells from cooking. The weight, also, of the crust pressing down on the doughy air-cells below, destroys them, — producing that horror of good cooks, a heavy streak. The problem in baking, then, is the quick application of heat, rather below than above the loaf, and its steady continuance till all the air-cells are thoroughly dried into permanent consistency. Every housewife must watch her own oven to know how this can be best accomplished."

"Cousin Kate, Miss Beecher says that after being put in the pans, the bread should stand not more than ten or fifteen minutes to rise, but you say an hour."

"Miss Beecher referred to bread which is allowed to rise in mass, after all the flour is in; and which is kneaded the last time only just enough to shape it into loaves; but in this bread which we are now baking, we dispense with this last moulding, as I think the bread sweeter without it. In the earlier stages of the process there is no danger of working bread too much; but, after all the flour is in, and has been well worked and perfectly fermented, the less it is manipulated and the sooner it is put to bake, the better."

"Cousin Kate, why do you prefer these small pans for baking, to a large pan, which would hold all four of the loaves?"

"For the reason given in the extract just read, that 'the excellence of bread depends on the perfection of its air-cells, that one of the objects of baking is to fix these air-cells, and that the quicker this can be done through the whole mass, the better will the result be.'

"Therefore, bake in small loaves, and let the loaf touch the pan at all points,—not another loaf. I have another reason, because it gives more crust; and crust is not only palatable, but a physiological necessity. Remember that many a good thing is spoiled in the oven, and when you put the bread in the pans to rise, look after the range fire."

"Cousin Kate, to return to the bread which is

rising, how am I to know when that critical moment of perfect and exact lightness has come? You have warned me against putting it to bake too soon, and cautioned me not to allow it to stand too long. Miss Beecher has also discoursed eloquently upon this fine point; but neither you nor she has explained the signs and signals that shall proclaim, 'Behold, this bread is at the supreme moment of its existence; it has risen to its best and highest point of perfection.'"

"That, Alice, is a difficult thing to do, so much depends upon the close observation and fine discrimination of the baker. But when you put bread in the condition of this into the pans, notice the size of the loaf, and allow it in rising to double its bulk. When light, if you press your finger gently upon the top of the loaf it will feel soft and spongy beneath. Press it away slightly from the side of the pan in such manner that you can see the texture or grain, and, if it looks light, put it into the oven; for I would have it bake while rising toward perfection unattained, rather than after having fallen from grace. The taste of the first suggests a better state as possible; while that of the last is hopelessly flat, stale, and unprofitable.

"The bread should be in the oven ten or fifteen minutes before it shows any little brown spots on its surface; and if these appear too soon, lessen the heat,— not by opening the oven-door, but by regulating the damper and draughts of the range. If the bread is not over light when put in the oven, it had better bake too slowly at first than too quickly; and the heat should be greatest under the loaf.

"It is highly important that the heat of the oven should be just right when the bread is put in it; for if it bakes too quickly, it will not rise properly, and if it bakes too slowly it will lack character and sweetness. Close observation, however, will very soon enable any one to decide when the oven is at right heat.

"When the bread is baked, the heat of the oven should decrease gradually, so that the last of the baking may be done very moderately. Be careful not to remove the bread from the oven until it is well done, or perfectly 'soaked,' as the Southern cooks say. When done, the crust should be firm, and equally brown all over. It should be a rich russet-gold, on the verge of a browner tinge, — not that pale, sickly hue suggesting a dull fire, and general dilapidation. To determine if bread is done, wet your finger, and touch the bottom of the pan outside; if it hisses, the bread is done, unless it has baked too rapidly.

"My grandmother's test was to touch the bottom of the loaf to the end of her nose; if it burned her nose, the bread was not done. But you can judge best from the length of time it has been in the oven, and from its lightness, whether or not bread is thoroughly baked. A loaf six inches thick should bake an hour, and thinner loaves in proportion; and a loaf of bread is much lighter after than before it is well-baked. Always bake small, thin loaves, unless forced to economize oven-room, as they are sweeter than larger ones. For this reason braided bread, or French twist, is a desirable form of loaf.

"For the twist, take a piece of dough the size of a small loaf, and bring it into a long loaf shape, pointing it at the ends by giving them an extra pressure or rolling; then, with a rolling-pin, flatten it like a pie-crust, rolling back and forth lengthwise, as it must be much longer than it is wide. Leave it an inch in thickness, and, with a a sharp knife, cut it lengthwise into three strips of equal width. Leave these strips unseparated at the end farthest from you, and carefully plait or braid them, pinching the ends well together. Lift the twist with care, and place it in a pan large enough to hold it without crushing or marring its form. If the dough is not allowed to get cold and is properly covered, such twists will rise in fifteen or twenty minutes; but remember, they should be lighter than bread. If not baked too brown, they will heat over nicely, by being placed for a few minutes in a hot oven and allowed to heat thoroughly, to the extent of taking on a browner tinge. A twist reheated I think better than one newly baked; but a twist dried for half an hour in a warm oven is another thing. Many cooks bake twists too lightly; all bread is more digestible well baked.

"Upon removing bread from the oven, take it out of the pans and tilt it against something upon the table, leaving as much of the surface exposed to the air as possible. Turn it after a few minutes, lest it sweat and soften where it rests. Cover it with nothing so long as it is too hot to be molested by flies; and, as it cools, if necessary, throw over it a very light bread-cloth. When quite cold, put it into a bread-box, which should be of tin, or wood lined with zinc,— in a square form, and with a convenient cover. Do not keep bread in the cellar or other damp place, nor in a closet where there is the odor of preserves or pickles. Taken care of in this way, bread will keep perfectly for several days, and I think is better the second or third day after baking than the day it is baked. Never allow loaves of bread to be cut while warm; for such use, bake in rolls or French twists, and be very careful to have the bread-box emptied of all stale pieces or crumbs, and perfectly clean and dry when the new bread is put away. But this will suffice for our lesson to-day."

CHAPTER III.

STILL DABBLING IN DOUGH.

"To-day, Alice, we will make rolls and Graham bread. Let us begin with Graham bread. Having set the ferment last night, we now divide it, pouring a portion into a separate bowl, into which we stir Graham flour, adding more or less sugar, according to taste, and a little salt. Add flour, in small quantities at a time, and allow the sponge to rise during the intervals. When too stiff to stir readily, work well with the hand until the dough seems very elastic and clinging. Add, at this working, all the flour required. When stiff enough, the dough will work free from the sides of the bowl; but Graham bread should be made less stiff than white bread. Leave it in the bowl to rise; and, when light, knead it upon the board only enough to shape into loaves, and then put it in pans to rise.

"It is well to gash all loaves of bread with a sharp knife, after they are in the pan. This incision should be an inch deep, and extend nearly the length of the loaf. This prevents binding, and allows the loaf, in rising, more freedom to shape itself gracefully. Put into warm pans, well covered, in a warm room, these Graham loaves will rise in twenty or thirty minutes; possibly fifteen. Graham bread does not require quite so hot an oven as white bread, but should bake a longer time.

"For rolls we have here a quart or three pints of ferment, into which we stir flour, the same as for bread. In every case be careful to have the flour warm, so that the fermentation may not be checked. Should you, at any time, find the ferment or sponge has received a chill, and is slow in its action, add the necessary warmth, not by placing it over a hot range, or close to the stove, where the heat will be extreme at some points, but by putting the bowl containing the sponge in a pan of warm water, and stirring it until the whole mass of dough becomes of an even temperature. When this roll-sponge is thick enough to be worked by the hand, add to it an ounce of butter, or lard, for each pint of ferment. If you desire to have rolls light and spongy, work them at least half an hour in the bowl, adding flour very gradually. Then place the dough upon the moulding-board and knead it well, adding flour only as is necessary to prevent it from sticking to the board and hands. The appearance of blisters upon the dough is an indication that it is well worked. Having washed and warmed the bowl, and greased it with sweet lard or butter, return the dough to it, and let it rise. When light, loosen the dough from the edge of the bowl and it will come out clean. If the greasing is omitted, the dough adheres, and must be scraped from the bowl and then rubbed from the fingers by means of flour. This covers the moulding-board with little hard wads, unfit to be worked into bread at this stage.

"Bring the dough quickly, with a few pressures, into a compact roll, and lay it aside. Cut from it a piece the size of a small loaf, and divide this into eight or ten parts; mould each in a round shape; and then, by rolling quickly back and forth under your hands, bring it into a long roll-form. Give the ends an extra roll, which points them slightly. Place at one end of the bread-pan, and proceed in like manner to fill the pan with rolls. It is well to flour the sides of the rolls where they touch each other, as that will keep them from running together; and, when baked, they are easily separated. Cover, and when very light, bake the same as twist. They are nice reheated. To ascertain if they are done, test them the same as bread; and if you are still in doubt, separate one from its fellows and press the finger against the soft part. If it retain the impression of the finger, it is not done. When baked sufficiently, all bread, when the finger is pressed against it, will rebound as soon as the pressure is withdrawn.

"When you wish to astonish your friends with a marvel of delicate lightness in rolls, add to the dough, when worked nearly enough to go on the moulding-board, the whites of three or four eggs, beaten to a stiff froth, and an additional half-ounce of butter for each egg. The butter should be worked in first; the eggs later, and a little at a time, alternating with flour. If eaten the same day they are baked, these rolls are more delicate, being lighter, more spongy, and whiter, than without the egg; but they are also richer, and do not keep so well. In making egg-rolls, work them almost entirely in the bowl, for they must remain too soft to be long worked on the board. The bread we have already baked is the kind preferred by most people, being light, spongy, and sweet. For eating when fresh, for making into milk toast, bread puddings, or griddle-cakes, and for crumbs with which to scallop or fry oysters, perhaps it is better for the spongy quality; but to a lover of bread and butter, pure and simple, bread made in the same manner, without potato, is best. It is light, but firmer and more compact in texture, and has a crisp sweetness excelling the other. In dry toast it is far better, having none of that husky emptiness which is a characteristic of dry toast made from spongy bread. Good bread may be made without potato, with very little labor. Beating it for a moment whenever flour is added, it need receive no other attention until stiff enough to be worked with the hand, when all the flour required can be worked in, during fifteen minutes' kneading, and the bread be placed immediately in the pans to rise. Make in this manner, and given only this small amount of time and labor, it will be found vastly superior to the bread at present disgracing a large proportion of American tables."

"Cousin Kate, why do you scald the flour with which you set the ferment for bread?"

"After trying various methods, I obtained the best results from so doing. Rising more slowly at first, the ferment appears to be quicker and more active, when its strength is most required to lighten the mass of flour. The scalding also prevents the ferment from souring; and it can, after becoming light, stand for hours without acquiring that yeasty smell and taste which spoil so much bread. But I have found, Alice, that to add flour, or remould just before the ferment or sponge attains its lightest stage, is always best; for if it passes that stage a moment, and 'falls' or 'settles,' something of sweetness and perfection is lost, that no care or labor can restore."

"Why do you use the wooden stick or spatula, instead of a spoon, for beating the sponge?"

"For several reasons. One is, that it is lighter; and the handle being round and smooth, does not fret the hand like metal. Then, it cuts through the dough more effectually than a spoon. My grandmother's hasty-pudding stick was the model after which this was made. It is well to have several of these in a house. They should be made of various sizes, of hickory, ash, or other hard wood, and should be from a foot and a half to two feet long. The blade should be from one and a half to two and a half inches in width, and four or five in length, thickest in the middle, gradually growing thin toward the edges, and square at the bottom. This stick is preferable to a spoon for beating cake or stirring mushes, and is quite indispensable in the fruit season, to keep small fruits stirred from the bottom of the preserving-kettle while cooking."

"Cousin Kate, all the cook-books that I have seen agree that milk is better than water for making bread. Why do you not use it?"

"For the reason that I differ in opinion from those who think milk best. Milk that stands and ferments, usually acquires an unpleasant smell and taste. Sponge made with milk is more likely to sour; and bread made with milk, at the same time that it is less sweet in flavor, dries sooner, and does not keep so well. Lastly, water is cheaper, and within the reach of all. The ferment for next day's baking can be set at any time during the afternoon or evening, except in hot weather, when it is better to start it about eight or nine o'clock in the evening."

"You don't seem to have much faith in the efficacy of soda in baking and cooking?"

"Soda, as used in many households, is one of the greatest abominations of the kitchen. It is a malign intruder in all mixtures where an acid is wanting; and even where an acid is present, it should be used with great care and discretion. The introduction of baking-powders is a good thing; for in these the acid and the alkali are more accurately proportioned than by careless cooks. Whenever I speak of a measure of baking-powder, I mean to designate the amount which the maker of the powder directs to be used in a given quantity of flour. Those baking-powders which are put up in separate parcels — the one containing the alkali, the other the acid — are perhaps preferable, but should only be used by cooks who believe in careful and exact measurements. In some cases, tin measures accompany the powder; in others, a teaspoon is the measure designated. To attain exactness in these measurements, place a portion of the powder on the moulding-board, and, with a knife, mash it smooth; then, fill the measure heaping full, and, with the knife, strike off all above the rim. Where exactness is indispensable, make even (never heaping) measures. Mix the quantity to be used with a small portion of flour by repeated siftings, which can be easily and quickly accomplished by the use of two pieces of strong soft paper. Place the sieve on one of these, and empty the flour from the other into it; shake through, and repeat as often as desirable. In all batter-cakes or soft dough, where baking-powder is used, mix it in this manner with a small quantity of flour, which add near the close of the mixing process; but in biscuit and stiff dough, sift the baking-powder through all the flour used. Some cooks are affected with soda mania. On general principles, as it seems, they put soda in all breads and cakes. If not required to sweeten or make light, they confidently assert it will make tender. So the greens are plagued, the string-beans tormented, and the young pease cursed, by this evil spirit, the exorcism of which would be a blessing to thousands.

"For lunch to-day, Alice, you shall make some cream biscuit which will take your mamma captive, and charm her as completely as any material substance can, if the biscuits you produce rival, as I hope they may, the puffy things made by my rosy-checked friend, Sally. Sally and I were girls together, and much of my summer rest was found at the old farm-house, where she and her sisters grew up, blossomed, and faded, as the years went by, in which I served my State as instructor of its youth. Through all my life, in which, I am sorry to say, hot biscuits have been a not infrequent event, I have never found any that quite equalled Sally's. She, however, was the only one in the family who invariably made them just right. If her mother or one of her sisters undertook the task, the cakes often came out of the oven yellow, and smelling of soda because of an overdose; or white and 'sad,' because too little had been used; for the exact amount required depended upon the acidity of the cream. Sally had the knack of guessing just right. Taking the bowl of sour cream in her hand, she would stir and taste it with a critical air; and giving a wise little nod, as if she had solved the riddle, proceed to measure a teaspoon, half full, even full, or heaping full, of soda, which she placed in a cup, and poured on it a spoonful of boiling water. Letting this stand, she made room in the middle of the flour for the cream; and, with her fingers, mixed the flour nearest the cream lightly in, adding a pinch of salt. While it was still a soft batter, she drained into it the soda, leaving any sediment there might be in the cup. Then her hands danced here and there through the dough, mixing it rapidly until stiff enough to roll out on the bread-board, cut into round cakes, and place immediately in a quick oven. In twenty minutes these cakes came out of the oven four times as thick as they went in, the most delicate, puffy things imaginable; but *your* cream biscuit, Alice, must be made with sweet milk and a little butter, instead of cream.

"To a quart of flour, add a measure of baking-powder, sifting the whole three or four times, and two ounces of butter, so carefully rubbed through the flour that you cannot find a particle the size of a pin-head. Add cold sweet milk, to make a soft dough; roll out, cut into cakes, and bake in a quick oven."

At lunch, Cousin Emeline praised the biscuits as she ate them with strawberries, which had been sprinkled with sugar, and set in the refrigerator for half an hour. The sugar, with its sweet art, had coaxed enough juice from the berries to dissolve itself; and, wrapped in this delicious syrup, the berries were far more palatable than when eaten sharply acid, with a portion of dry sugar. Alice was pleased with the praise her mother bestowed upon the biscuit, until it occurred to her that even a higher achievement had been possible. Then she asked, half reproachfully,—

"Cousin Kate, why did you not have me make a strawberry shortcake,— or don't you know how?"

"Oh, yes. You would make the shortcake just

like these biscuits; roll the dough quite thin, not much thicker than pie-crust, and baking on pie-pans, the size of the pan. When baked, with a fork and your fingers separate the upper and under crust of the cake, spread the inside with butter, and laying one-half of the cake on a plate, cover it thickly with berries, well sprinkled with sugar. Then add another half cake and another layer of berries, till the pie is thick enough, finishing with fruit. If you desire to disguise, and, in a measure, destroy the flavor of the berry, serve strawberry shortcake with sweet cream poured over it. The cream also renders it more indigestible. My opinion is, that any one, after eating sweet, crisp loaf-bread, a day old, with strawberries served like these, will never voluntarily run the risk of dyspepsia, for the sake of hot biscuit or strawberry shortcake.

"Belonging to the bread family, and a very genuine, respectable member thereof, is our round, chubby little travelling companion, known as 'Maryland Biscuit.' Although rarely met with outside the State whose name it bears, it is a very desirable acquaintance for travellers who provide their own lunches; for picnic parties, and for ladies who desire always to have the pantry well stored with good things. The Maryland biscuit occupies that happy medium state between a cracker and an ordinary biscuit or roll, and is by many preferred to either. To bring these cakes out of the oven perfect specimens of their kind, requires some labor, as it is necessary not only to knead, but also to pound or beat them with a heavy hammer or mallet. To four pints of flour add three ounces of lard, a teaspoonful of salt, and a pint of cold water. Rub the lard and salt through the flour until perfectly mixed, before adding the water. This proportion of water may not be the exact quantity in all cases, as some flour requires more, some less; but the dough must be very stiff, and rendered soft and pliable by working and pounding. When light, and well worked, the dough will 'blister,' and pulling off a small piece quickly will cause a sharp, snapping sound. When these signs appear, rest from the labor of pounding; gather between your fingers a little wad of the dough, pull it suddenly from the main lump, and, moulding it into a round mass, lay aside, face downward. In like manner fashion enough to fill the bread-pan. Then, one by one, pick up these round balls, and hold each for an instant in the hollow of your left hand. While nestled there so cozily, place your right thumb squarely in its face, enlarging equally its surface, and leaving a hollow in the centre; place in the bread-pan, not allowing the biscuits to touch each other. Prick them with a fork. Bake at once in a hot oven until done, and of a light brown color.

If the cakes are 'sad,' or heavy inside, when cold, they are not sufficiently baked, as they should be light, and of a fine, even grain. When most perfect, these biscuits crack at the edges or sides, the upper and under crust being forced apart, in order to give a hint of the lightness and whiteness within. When your oven is sufficiently hot, twenty minutes is about the average time required to bake them properly.

"No Maryland supper-table is in company order without these modest, unpretending little fellows, who are quite at home with fried oysters, and fit company for cold turkey and broiled chicken."

One morning at breakfast, Alice asked, "When may I be queen of the kitchen for a whole week, and do all the cooking without any supervision, Cousin Kate? I shall not feel really certain that I know how to cook so long as you have to oversee me. Besides, when are you to write that lecture on 'The Proper Rearing and Training of Children,' if you devote all your time to me and the kitchen?"

After reflecting a moment, I replied, "Your suggestion is a good one, Alice, and this plan occurs to me: For one week I will do the cooking, and you shall observe and help as heretofore; and, during the week, you shall note the bill of fare at each meal, and make such memoranda as you think necessary. Then, the week following, you may repeat or duplicate my week of cooking."

"I like that proposition," said Alice: and Emeline added, "I hope you'll make a judicious selection, Kate, if we are to repeat the bill of fare,— good, bad, or indifferent."

The next day I began on the preparatory week, and on the evening of the seventh day thereafter, I abdicated in favor of Alice, who brought her note-book, and, while finding the place, murmured, "For breakfast one week ago to-morrow morning, we had — oh, here it is — oatmeal mush, picked-up codfish cooked with cream, baked potatoes, French twist reheated, coffee. *Mem.* — At seven o'clock, when I entered the kitchen, Cousin Kate stood by the long table, knife in hand, bending over a codfish. She stripped off large pieces of the fish, then cut them across the grain, into pieces an inch long. As these were two or three inches wide, she picked them into small bits, throwing out the bones, and letting the fish fall into a pan of cold water. In a few minutes she had thus prepared enough for breakfast. Stirring it about in the water, she left it to freshen, while she prepared the oatmeal mush. Into a tin-lined stew-pan she put two pints of water and half a teaspoonful of salt. When the water boiled, she sprinkled in, slowly, half a pint of oatmeal, stirring it with the mush-stick. The water was boiling quite rapidly. In two minutes the meal was all in, but she continued to stir, letting it boil for two or three minutes longer, when it appeared about the consistency of thick gruel or thin batter. Then she placed the stewpan back on the range, where the heat was only enough to keep it simmering. Removing the stick and covering closely, she left it undisturbed till breakfast. Next, she took six potatoes of medium size, and, washing them very clean, placed them in a pan ready for the oven. Then she ground the coffee and put it to steep, not boil. She allowed a tablespoonful of coffee for each cup; and, placing it in the pot, added a cup of cold water, and set it back on the range to steep. If it chanced to boil, she added more cold water. Just before serving breakfast, she added as much boiling water as was needed, and allowed it to boil for a minute; then she lifted the pot to the kitchen table, and with a spoon removed the grounds which adhered to the inside of the pot, near the top. Rinsing these off, she poured out part of a cup, which she put immediately back, added a spoonful of cold water, and sent the coffee to the breakfast-table. When mamma poured it, three minutes later, it was clear as amber. Cousin Kate selected a bowl-shaped iron kettle holding about two quarts, and not a shallow pan or spider, in which to cook the codfish. She stirred the fish about in the water, and drained it in a tin strainer. then placed it in the kettle with half a pint of fresh water, covered it close, and let it boil for ten minutes, or until the water was all evaporated, and the fish well cooked. At this stage she added a pint of thin cream; and when it boiled, two spoonfuls of flour stirred to a smooth paste in a little cold milk, let it boil for a minute or two, peppered it lightly, and served it. About ten minutes before breakfast, she put the twist into the oven; and, from time to time, looked at it to be sure it was not burning. When the potatoes were baked, breakfast was served immediately. Cousin Kate lifted the pan containing them to the kitchen table; then, one by one, picked up the potatoes in a cloth, which she held to protect her hand, gave each a gentle squeeze, until opened its mouth, whence issued a puff of hot air; then placing them in a dish, sent them to the table."

When Alice had finished reading these notes from her memorandum book, I said, "Correct, to the minutest particular." She smilingly answered, as she bade me good-night, "Then let not your heart be troubled about breakfast, nor have a thought of care or responsibility. I shall ring the dressing-bell at half-past seven, and woe betide you and mamma, if you spoil my first breakfast by your tardiness."

Cousin Emeline and I were on time next morning, and presented our queen of the kitchen with a bouquet of freshly-gathered flowers, in the arrangement of which we had spent some anxious moments. As I served the codfish (white, creamy, and tempting), I said, "Now *this* fills the spoon in a plump and satisfactory manner. I am very fond of codfish when properly cooked; and I find it terribly trying, sometimes, to have so appetizing a dish fraudulently represented by bits of fish half-cooked, and salt as brine, straying forlornly about in a sloppy gravy. But this is just right; neither too thick nor too thin. In this artistic combination, it is difficult to decide where the fish ends, and where the gravy begins."

Here Emeline interrupted my rhapsody over the fish, by asking, "Where is the boiled milk for Kate's coffee, Alice?"

"There! I've forgotten the milk. But how did it happen that it was not down in my memoranda?"

"For the reason, I dare say, that boiling milk in a milk-boiler requires very little attention. You fill the inner boiler with milk and the outer one with water, and set it back on the range, where it simmers and sings to itself, until needed; and I suppose you neglected to make note of so trifling a matter."

"I am very sorry, indeed, Cousin Kate; for to weaken your coffee with water will spoil it."

"Not at all, when I have cream like this. But

isn't it strange, Emeline, that so indispensable a thing as a milk-boiler should be so rarely found in the kitchen?— and that the mistress of the house should go on, year after year, boiling milk in all sorts of pots and pans,— often scorching it so that it is unfit for use, wasting the milk, and spoiling her temper, all for the want of a milk-boiler which costs a dollar?"

"But supposing, Kate, she hasn't got the dollar, and if she asks her husband for it, he answers with contempt, 'Milk-boiler, indeed! My *mother* was one of the best cooks in the world, and she never heard of a milk-boiler!' What would you do in such a crisis, Kate?" "I don't know; but I have serious thoughts now, of writing a lecture, as soon as the one about children is finished, entitled, 'The Abuse of Power, or the Cause and Cure of Domestic Infelicity.' Here Alice laughed outright, saying, "Excuse me, Cousin, but it seems so funny that you who never had husband or child, should write upon these subjects."

"For that very reason, Alice, may I not be an impartial and unprejudiced observer? Commend me to an old maid or an old bachelor for true wisdom on these subjects."

Thus, in idle talk we whiled away an hour over Alice's first breakfast, which Emeline and I pronounced a success, notwithstanding the forgotten milk.

CHAPTER IV.

FOOD AND FANCY.

Emeline passed her plate for a second piece of chicken, remarking, as she did so, "These chickens that you and Alice fry must be a new kind, for so far as I can discover, they have neither backs, necks, legs, nor wings. Truly a valuable breed this must be, which runs entirely to breast and second joints; the frying kind, I suppose. But seriously, Kate, what do you do with the remainder of these fowls, and how do you cut such plump, compact little pieces, each one of which is a delicious surprise on a near acquaintance?"

I was thinking about another matter, and replied, "Cousin Emeline, in this cook-book of mine, I mean to devote one whole chapter to the consideration of suitability. I have a friend, the charming Mrs. Rose; you used to know her; a woman of fine native talent, rare culture, easy, affable manner, and great personal beauty. But her one charm, which with me outshines all others, is tact. She has tact more perfectly developed than any one I ever knew.

Prince or beggar feels alike at ease in her presence; but she would never think of inviting them to her house on the same occasion. If she is going to have a little supper-party of ten or a dozen, and her guests are invited to meet a friend who may be staying with her, she says to herself, 'Now here is Fanny, with such and such tastes. She is this order of person. I will invite those people to meet her who are harmonious; such as will call out her peculiar powers; some sharp contrasts. She goes to work in an artistic manner and selects her guests, having reference mainly to suitability. This same tact is called into exercise in deciding what her dinner or supper shall be. The principal dish determines what shall be its companions. But many women seem to lose sight entirely of this suitability of things, especially in eating. Such are just as likely to have griddle-cakes and fish for breakfast, as griddle-cakes and stewed chicken, or griddle-cakes and beefsteak."

"But to return to this chicken," said Emeline. "In all my travels, at home and abroad, I never tasted its equal. How is it prepared?"

"Why, you see, mamma," said Alice, "having fried chicken for dinner necessitates having stewed chicken for breakfast, either before or after, in order to use the other parts. But this is true economy, Cousin Kate says; for while the breast and second joints are best fried, the other parts are much better stewed, From the breast we get three nice frying pieces, so nearly alike that you can scarcely tell them apart. Having decided where to cut it, instead of sawing and haggling with a dull knife, and in the struggle mutilating the pieces so that they remind you of 'the ragged edge of despair,' Cousin Kate puts the breast of the chicken on the meat-board, and placing the knife just where she wishes to cut, strikes it a blow that sends the blade through the chicken at one clean stroke. Having washed the pieces and dried them on a soft towel, while the lard, of which there should be a liberal supply, is heating, we rub each piece of chicken lightly, with salt and pepper, which has been mixed together in suitable proportions, and just before dropping into the boiling lard, dust it with flour. To ascertain if the lard is hot enough, slip into it a slice of raw potato, and when the potato is brown, the lard is sufficiently heated. Drop into the boiling lard one piece of chicken at a time, and let the bubbling and tumult, incident to its reception, somewhat subside before adding another. When the pieces are of a rich brown color, they will be found well-cooked, and may be placed on a tin or wire strainer in a warm oven, until ready to serve. Chicken fried in this manner is much less greasy than when cooked in a small quantity of lard. Nearly all kinds of fresh fish are best fried in the same way. To parboil a chicken before frying, Cousin Kate says, is barbarous treatment, not of the chicken but of the people who eat it after it has been robbed of its best juices."

"Now, Alice, tell me how you make these Graham 'gems,' for I really think they deserve the name."

"To a pint each of cold, sweet milk and pure water, add a teaspoonful of sugar, a salt-spoonful of salt, and three pints of Graham flour. Sprinkle in the flour slowly, stirring the mixture rapidly, and when all is added beat the dough briskly for a minute or two before an open window or door; for Cousin Kate says, pure air is very essential to the life of bread, especially bread which is made light by beating. Bake the gems in iron gem-pans or puff-pans, half filling the cups which must be well heated and greased. Bake in a quick oven, the greatest heat being applied to the bottom when first put in the oven.

"Fine flour gems, or English muffins, are made in the same manner as Graham, omitting the sugar, and adding a pint more of flour. Gems are good made with water instead of milk and water.

"Very excellent Graham cakes are made by putting a teaspoonful of sugar and a salt-spoonful of salt into a quart of Graham flour, and pouring upon it boiling water, stirring it meanwhile until all is wet and soft enough to be worked into a mass resembling a large roll, or small loaf of bread. Work it as little as possible, and when brought into this shape, cut it with a sharp knife, dipped in flour, into slices half an inch thick. Place these in a bread-pan and bake in a hot oven for half an hour, or until brown. There, Cousin Kate, haven't I said my lesson well?"

"Perfectly. And having induced you, Alice, to make and taste these kinds of Graham bread, I am content, well knowing that you will push your investigations, and find by experiment that the varieties of delicious bread which can be made of Graham flour and water are almost numberless."

After a moment's pause Emeline renewed the conversation by saying, "Kate, I hope you will devote some space in your book to mushes; for, although not a lover of them myself, I discover a great difference in the appearance of oatmeal prepared by your method, and that usually served. And I notice that Alice eats your oatmeal with a relish, whereas heretofore she has seemed to eat all kinds of mushes from a sense of duty because they were recommended by her physician."

"What a close observer you are, mamma!" laughingly rejoined Alice. "But I own to liking Cousin Kate's hygienic mushes rather better than those which taste so decidedly of water. Hominy grits, as often served, in a half-raw state, taste as I imagine chicken-feed does. Crushed wheat when half cooked seems all bran. And underdone oatmeal is as disagreeable a mixture as I care to partake of."

"The misnomers of the past," I said, in reply to these observations, "cause us a great deal of suffering. For instance, some careless, slovenly cook, years ago, may have quickly boiled corn meal in water and named it "hasty pudding," and unthinking people, judging it is so called because little time is required to prepare it, go on from generation to generation eating half-boiled mush, or hasty pudding, without discovering that it is best when made in a manner the very reverse of hasty. Indeed, I know of no mush that is not better for much cooking; and slow cooking is also preferable, after all the meal has been stirred in. Many persons object to mushes because of the trouble of preparing, as the general opinion is that they require a special boiler, or must be constantly stirred. This, however, is a mistake. The double or jacketed boiler is no doubt most convenient for cooking mushes in; but a smooth, bowl-shaped, iron kettle, and a wooden stick or spatula will answer every purpose, and the process of making need not be at all laborious.

For oatmeal, and crushed or cracked wheat, I use the same proportions,—one measure of meal to four of water,—sprinkling the meal slowly into the water, which must be boiling, and stirring constantly. I continue the boiling and stirring, after the meal is all in, until the mush thickens enough to jump up and hop about in a lively manner. Then I remove the stick, cover the vessel closely, and set it where it will only simmer. An hour of this slow boiling or simmering renders oatmeal and crushed wheat mushes far superior to those made hastily by rapid boiling. Not only is the grain and texture different; but flavors, delicious and not discovered in mushes made rapidly, seem to be elicited from the grain by this quiet undisturbed simmering — especially is this the case with crushed wheat. And by the way, I think it is a mistaken impression that crushed wheat should only be eaten hot. To my taste, it is far more delicious cold, or nearly so.

"Many cooks complain of fine hominy or grits being troublesome to cook, because of its tendency to stick to the kettle, unless constantly stirred. But I find that greasing the kettle with lard or butter before putting the water in, seems to obviate the difficulty materially. Fine hominy requires five measures of water to one measure of hominy. It should be put into cold water, and allowed to swell for half an hour, before the water boils. While swelling it should be stirred every few minutes. As soon as it begins to boil, place it where it will boil rapidly for ten or fifteen minutes, or until it becomes the proper consistency, which should be the same as that of other mushes, when it can be set back, covered closely, and allowed to simmer for an hour. All kinds of mushes should be salted very slightly, and I think it better to put the salt in the water before stirring in the grain or meal. A majority of cooks spoil mushes by over-salting them."

"It must be to get rid of their briny taste that people who eat mushes generally destroy all their flavor by adding immense quantities of sugar or syrup," observed Emeline. "The idea never struck me before."

At breakfast next morning the stewed chicken was a failure, at which Alice was much mortified. She said, deprecatingly:

"Cousin Kate, it is not at all like yours, yet I was very careful to read up my notes, which said: 'Two chickens, minus the frying pieces, are equal to one whole chicken. To stew them, add one-half pint water, cover closely, and boil gently or simmer smartly, until very tender. Then drain from them the water, add a piece of butter, or the oil from the water you have drained out, let them brown nicely, turning the pieces when necessary.' That is what is the matter; I didn't brown the chicken. Who would suppose so small a thing would make so vast a difference?"

"This browning, Alice, changes the whole character of the dish, and makes rich and appetizing what is otherwise weak and vapid."

"Go on, Alice," said her mother; "give me the rest of the recipe."

"When browned, lift the chicken, and pour into the stew-pan the water previously drained out, having removed any surplus oil. When it boils, thicken with flour, stirred to a smooth paste in a little cold milk, or sweet cream. Make it thick enough to deserve the name of gravy, season with salt and pepper, and return the chicken to it, letting it remain in the stew-pan long enough to become thoroughly saturated. Dish chicken and gravy together."

"Kate," remarked Emeline, "I have been prejudiced all my life against stewed chicken, because the gravy was so inefficient,—such a wretchedly demoralized mixture, tasting a little of chicken and very much of water and raw flour. But stewed chicken, *a la* Cousin Kate, has my hearty approval. In England we sometimes found stewed chicken that was very nice. It was as this would be if you left out the cream and added some pickled mushrooms. Mushrooms give a delicious flavor to the dish."

"Beef, veal, and lamb, are all delicious when stewed in the same manner," I said to Alice. Then Emeline continued:

"Kate, I wonder why it is that women abhor the kitchen, and so detest pottering among pots and pans? You open this subject to me in a new light, and I lose sight of the drudgery and unpleasant work in my interest about results, and my inquiries after the cause. When we consider, there is nothing of greater importance than this question, What shall we eat, and how shall it be cooked? For what order of men and women we are, depends very much upon the food we eat. The world seems divided mainly into those who live to eat, and those who regard eating a troublesome and expensive necessity, but a nuisance. There are very few who eat to live in the truest sense."

"The trouble, Emeline, is, that people don't think; they go stumbling and groping through life because they haven't found out that their brains are for use. They never consider or think about these things. If mothers realized that the food their children eat has a positive quality; that it actually contains the principle of life or death, health or disease, they could not be so indifferent. Did they realize the vital importance of this matter, they would no sooner trust to a slovenly, unskilled cook the preparation of their children's food, than they would the washing of their expensive laces. Do they care more for their Honitons and Valenciennes than for their Toms and Marys? I think not. But one washing of a fine lace by a careless Bridget, reduces it to useless rags, whereas these living and breathing jewels are destroyed more slowly, and the mother does not see the wear and tear of bad food so palpably."

One evening Emeline and I were sitting on the western veranda watching the sunset, when Alice ran lightly up the steps. Her hat was in her hand, and her beautiful hair, unconfined by comb or plait, floated at will in wavy splendor. Her cheeks were glowing and her eyes sparkling as she spoke excitedly,

"Oh, mamma, I've had an adventure this evening. The air was exhilarating, the birds sang so gayly, and all nature seemed so blithe and happy, that I, too, took wing, and flew, rather than walked, this way and that, unheeding, in truth not caring, where the lovely crooked ways led me; until suddenly I came upon a small cottage by the roadside. It was nestled just under the hill, and was a very bird's-nest for coziness. I came upon it from the rear, through a garden all aglow with red roses and carnation-pinks, and had almost walked into the house before I realized what I was doing. The door stood open, and looking out at me amazed, as well they might be, were a pair of large brown eyes. So earnest and beseeching was their gaze that I stood spell-bound, like one dazed or in a dream. The owner of these marvellous eyes was a young girl who seemed an invalid, as she reclined on a lounge beside which the small supper-table was placed. Another lady sat at the table with her back toward me. A look or low-spoken word from the sick girl directed this lady's attention to me, and she came out and invited me in to rest. I didn't care to rest, but I did care to learn something of this brown-eyed beauty who seemed sick and sad. But no, I think I am wrong there; her eyes only had a wistful look, as if asking, pleading for something they dared not hope to gain; but her voice was cheerful and her laugh free and joyous. Yet she suffers a great deal, and has been for years confined to her lounge by some affection of the spine. Mamma, I think you made a mistake in writing your novel before I discovered this lovely heroine."

Emeline responded —

"By the way, Kate, did I tell you of 'My lord' and his mother whom we met last summer in Switzerland? We talked with them upon several occasions, yet did not learn their name or the land of their nativity. I thought them Americans from their manners and speech, but Alice insisted that they were English. She imagined him to be an English lord, 'the last of his race,' and that, she thought, accounted for their deep mourning and great dejection."

"No," I answered, while a vague suspicion

crossed my mind, "you have never spoken of them to me, but I am interested. Describe them more fully. What were they like in personal appearance?"

"Very much like each other, both having the same dark, deep eyes — eyes that remind you of bottomless wells of pure water, with shadows lingering about them hinting of sunshine. He was twenty-five or thirty years of age, and she old enough to be his mother. His hair was dark, and rippled or waved back from his forehead, while hers was so white that it reminded one of a fleecy cloud floating about her face."

"Was she slightly lame?" I asked.

"Yes," answered Emeline; "how came you to guess *that* grace belonged to her?"

"Perhaps my question was the offspring of your remembrance," I answered, evasively. "And Alice thought him a hero, did she? And in her visions of romance she has no doubt visited his ancestral home, his lordly domain? How is it, my dear, do you dream of him still?"

A rosy flush swept over her fair face as she answered:

"Indeed, Cousin Kate, I never dreamed of him but once in my life, and that was the first night I slept in this house. You remember it was after dark when we arrived, and to me it did seem a little weird and dismal for three lone women to take possession of a roomy old mansion like this, and although I wouldn't own it then, I was nervous and fidgety, starting at every sound all the evening. That I should dream strange dreams that night was a matter of course."

"But I never heard you mention this fact before, Alice," said her mother. "Pray tell us this strange dream."

"I would rather not," said Alice, blushing more deeply, "lest you think me a silly girl, and vain as foolish."

By this time Alice had really aroused our curiosity, and Cousin Emeline and I both protested that dreams were only dreams, and that we should not think of attaching any importance whatever to hers. Finally, we induced her to tell us her dream, in which she said she rehearsed the scene of our arrival at Maplewood, with this variation: she had lost sight of her mother and me, and entered the wide, gloomy hall alone. As she stepped timidly forward, she heard the great door close with a clang behind her, shutting her, like a prisoner, within. A wild terror seized her, and she was about to cry out for help, when a voice of exceeding sweetness said gently, "Welcome home, my darling." "I knew the voice," said Alice, 'and looking up, beheld 'My lord' descending the hall stair. But the curious part of the dream was that he bore in his arms a beautiful child, laughing and crowing with delight."

"Could that have been the boy Cupid, I wonder?" said I, teasingly; but Emeline seemed interested, and asked,

"What happened next, Alice? What did you say or do?"

"I guess I ran away, for I remember no more."

A few days after this conversation, I stood by a table in the large old kitchen beside Alice, who was earnestly engaged writing out my recipe for buns. The summer breeze played idly with her brown curls, while the delicious odor of the freshly-baked buns, mingled with that of the wild-rose and honeysuckle, making a confusion of sweet perfumes. At length, laying down the pen, she said,

"Cousin Kate, I want to take some of these airy things (the buns) to Jessie James this evening, with a basket of the brightest, sweetest strawberries Mike can find in the garden. May I?"

I bowed assent, and she went on,

"Jessie knows all about your friends, the Douglases, and has promised to tell me about his beautiful young wife, whose sudden death almost broke the heart of her husband."

Looking up from my work, I said,

"*Whose* beautiful young wife? What *are* you talking about, Alice?"

"About Gerald Douglas, whose wife died so suddenly just before they went abroad. Jessie says that was the reason of their going, and that his mother is devoted to him, and would go with him to the ends of the earth, if he desired."

"Very likely," I replied; "most mothers would do the same."

"But why, Cousin Kate, did you never tell me of this only son of your old friend?"

"Why, bless me, child, when and why, pray, should I have told you the history of this particular young man? Have you not been for years abroad, and before that, close shut within the walls of the 'Sacred Heart,' conning your lessons ever since you were a child? Never, until now, Alice, did I realize what a fearful responsibility rests upon a maiden lady whose old friend and schoolmate happens to have a terrible only son. Ah, woe is me!"

"Now Cousin Kate, please don't laugh at me, but shut up here with only your cook-book and mamma's novel to think about, is it strange that I like to hear Jessie tell of these people? Indeed, I think it would be very ungrateful not to be interested in them, since we've taken possession of their beautiful home and all their lovely things, just as if they belonged to us. Jessie says that the family portraits are in the drawing-room, and that the suite of rooms in the north wing belonged to his wife, and were fitted up according to her taste when she came here a bride; and that they are kept just as she left them. Would you mind asking Susannah to show them to us some time, when she opens to air and dust them; or do you think she would object?"

"Oh, no! Susannah will be only too glad to show you all her treasures, and I will ask her some day. But we must give some attention to the realities of the culinary department before we wander into the fields of romance."

CHAPTER V.

GRIDDLE-CAKES AND OTHER THINGS.

"Kate, I wonder if we shall be permitted to go on in this quiet, restful way all summer? I never enjoyed anything so much; but am all the while haunted by the fear that some prowling interloper will discover our retreat. Do you not think Alice wanders about too unguardedly, and is making too many acquaintances?"

I had barely time to respond "Nonsense, Emeline," when the little silver bell tinkled a summons to breakfast. Leaving the roses ungathered, we went in, to find a vase of them already upon the breakfast-table, mingling their sweet odors with those of more substantial things.

When Alice, with a little air of pride, passed the cakes to me—such perfectly formed, dainty-looking things—the sight of them somehow called from their graves a spectral army of ghostly cakes, the cakes of other days, and of less careful cooks than our charming Alice. Haunted by their memory, I said to Emeline, "What an abomination the griddle is in most houses, filling them with stifling atmospheres and unsavory odors. And yet it is easy to avoid both smoke and smell. Cakes may be baked in the kitchen, and no one up-stairs be wiser or sadder therefor, if the cook knows how to tend the griddle. But if she floods it with grease, which is allowed to burn before the cakes are placed upon it, not only is the house filled with smoke, but the cakes are blackened, and to a great extent spoiled, coming to the table with lacerated edges, bruised and torn, in their fierce conflict with fat and fire. Many cooks seem to take a special delight in causing the smoke of their torment, the griddle, to ascend unceasingly; and to this end they deluge it with grease, which, by the time it is filled with cakes, has been crowded close to the edges, where it hisses and bubbles, sputtering angrily all through the baking. Here and there on the griddle are drops of batter, impromptu little cakes undesigned by the cook, to which she pays no heed, unless, when lifting their more important kindred, she gives them an impatient push into the gutter of grease at the edge of the griddle, where they fry and burn uncared for. Sometimes it happens that these vagrants, black and dismal as they appear, are caught up accidentally and mixed with the cakes sent to the table. But oftener they are pushed off the griddle upon the range, where their illegitimate lives end in smoke."

"But, Kate, how is this nuisance to be prevented?"

"By using a suitable greaser in a proper manner. A good greaser may be made of pure lard placed just where it is required, by means of a linen swab, fastened to the end of a stick fashioned for the purpose; but the best greaser is a piece of fat pork, two inches square and an inch thick, with the rind covering one of its broadest surfaces. Slip this piece of pork on a fork in such a manner as to bring the tines of the fork close to the rind, leaving the greaser below. With this rub the griddle where the cakes are to be placed, wiping it well with a dry cloth after each baking. A griddle so treated will annoy no one, not even the cook, with smoke. Griddles and bread-pans should be used for nothing but the purpose for which they are specially designed, and should very rarely be washed with soap. If kept clean, they need little washing at any time, as a brisk rubbing with a dry cloth when they are warm is all-sufficient, and keeps them in more perfect condition than frequent washing."

"Using soapstone, and other griddles which require no grease, is the most sensible way of abating the griddle nuisance, I think," said Emeline.

"No doubt you are right," I replied. "Still, there are people who will cling to the old ways, notwithstanding the new have been proven to be best."

"Buckwheat-cakes are perhaps more universally eaten in this country than any other kind, and at the same time are more invariably and unmitigatedly bad. A mean buckwheat-cake suggests the idea of total depravity in cakes. Imagine a Christian gentleman breakfasting on those tawny, leaden things,—leathery, gritty, sour, and half raw. In eating them, he forfeits a good share of self-respect, and goes his way after breakfast with a heavy heart in his bosom and a bitter taste in his mouth. If he did not know he was the victim of buckwheat-cakes he would be morally certain the whole world was against him, and his best friend had become his worst enemy.

"A buckwheat-cake at its best is certainly queen of the griddle, a very princess among cakes,—light, brown, crisp. It has no ragged edge, no tawny, leaden-gray color, streaked with black. Sour? Why, the smoke of it is as grateful as sweet incense. You pat it tenderly with your knife, then spread it daintily with the sweet butter waiting to be gracious, adding syrup just to make the honeycomb illusion complete. I never knew a man after breakfasting on such cakes to contemplate suicide, or grumble even if his wife asked him for money."

Here Emeline interrupted me with,—

"Kate, why don't you have Alice keep pencil and paper at hand to jot down such little impromptu speeches for your cook-book? My opinion is that some of the best thoughts and choicest sayings of writers never get into their books. They come and go, with the passing moment of inspiration, known only to the fortunate few who happen to be at table, or in the drawing-room. But are you aware, that at the beginning of breakfast I asked you what kind of cakes these are that we are eating?"

"Is it possible you don't know?"

"All things are possible, it seems, when you and Alice play your witcheries in the kitchen; but, although I'm not sure, I think they are rice-cakes. Rice-cakes are my favorite cakes, and these are certainly very nice."

Here Alice's musical laugh rippled into the conversation with,—

"Rice-cakes, indeed, mamma; you ought to have seen the stale old bread that went to make up these little brown beauties."

Emeline answered with indignation, not unmixed with disgust,—

"Bread-cakes, Alice, are my particular detestation,— soft, sticky, and disagreeable."

"Oh fie, mamma! how shocking! But I hasten to heap coals of fire on your head, by giving you the exact recipe for these delicate, delicious cakes: Pour over a pint of bread-crumbs, the same measure of boiling milk. If the milk has been skimmed, a small piece of butter must be added. Cover closely, and let stand over night. In the morning mash to a smooth paste, and beat thoroughly with it the yolks of two eggs. Then gradually add half a pint of cold milk, beating meanwhile, and half a pint of flour with which a measure of baking-powder has been sifted. Lastly, add the whites of the eggs, beaten to a stiff froth. These cakes require longer baking than batter-cakes, and should be baked of a small size, as they are tender and easily torn, and, when served, should be spread over the plate, and not piled one upon the other."

"Rice-cakes, Alice, may be made in the same manner as bread-cakes, substituting well-boiled rice for bread-crumbs."

"And how are waffles made, Cousin Kate?" asked Alice.

"This is an excellent recipe for a simple raised waffle: One quart of milk, one ounce of butter, three pints of flour, and half a gill of yeast. Let rise over night. In making waffles, or batter-cakes that rise over night, I think it best to heat the milk to boiling point, adding to it, while hot, the butter or lard to be used. When cool enough to not scald the flour, add that; then the eggs, well beaten; and lastly the yeast. Give all a thorough beating. As soon in the morning as convenient, give the batter a good beating. This will add to the lightness and excellence of the cakes.

"The proportion of three pints of flour to a quart of milk, which you see is a measure and a half of flour to a measure of milk, I find to be the average proportions required in all kinds of batter-cakes; but the exact quantity of flour must be determined by the number of eggs and the amount of butter used. Where many eggs are used, less flour is needed, unless a great quantity of butter or lard, also, is used.

"Now, I will give you two more recipes for waffles, both excellent, which illustrate my meaning: One quart of milk, three pints of flour, four ounces of lard, four ounces of butter, six eggs, half a gill of yeast. In this recipe I should make no deduction of flour on account of the eggs used, because of the quantity of butter and lard. But in this: One quart of milk, three pints of flour, four eggs, and four ounces of butter, I should take light measure of flour. Flour should always be sifted before it is measured, and the measure should not be heaped. These last waffles are very nice, and are made in this manner: Add the flour to the cold milk, and beat thoroughly. Melt the butter, and add by degrees. Separate the eggs, adding one yolk at a time, and beating it thoroughly into the batter, before adding another. Lastly, add the whites, beaten to a stiff froth.

Bake immediately. If well beaten, these are good either as waffles or griddle-cakes. This recipe is also very nice when made over night, and raised with a gill of yeast. In that case, add butter and eggs in the morning. And you can also vary, by sometimes using baking-powder. As a general rule, in making all kinds of batter-cakes, beat the yolks of the eggs with the batter, and the whites separately, adding them last.

"Here is a flannel-cake that is simple, but very nice. Take equal portions of fine corn meal and wheat-flour. To a quart of warm water add three pints of meal and flour mixed, a pinch of salt, and half a gill of yeast. Let rise over night.

"For muffins, take a quart of milk, two quarts of flour, and a measure of baking-powder. Beat all thoroughly together, and bake in muffin-rings, or puff-pans, in a quick oven.

"The varieties of waffles, griddle-cakes, muffins, etc., are very numerous. But any one knowing how to make a few, can, without a cook-book, find out, by a little reflection, how to make numberless others."

"But Kate," said Emeline, "I wish to know how those queenly buckwheat cakes are made. Most housekeepers have difficulty with their 'buckwheats.' They are either too thick or too thin; and when not actually sour, have a strong, rank taste. I have never found in any cook-book the proportions of flour and water to be used in making buckwheat cakes. This important item is left to the judgment or discretion of the cook. Do you know the exact proportions?"

"My favorite buckwheat cakes are made in this manner: Make two quarts of gruel, by adding to two quarts of boiling water half a pint of corn meal, wet with a little cold water; boil well. Then cool to lukewarmness and add half a pint of wheat flour, three pints of buckwheat flour, one gill of yeast, and salt to taste. Set in a moderately warm place until perfectly light.

"Buckwheat cakes should be set to rise at noon, for the next morning, and by eight or nine o'clock they will be light, when they should be well beaten and set in a cool place through the night.

"Just before baking, add a little soda if needed, and thin by adding a little warm water if necessary."

"I observe," said Alice, "that in these buckwheat cakes which have no eggs, you use only a measure of flour to a measure of water, while in wheat flour cakes, you use a measure and a half of flour. Why is that?"

"The nature of the grain is different; buckwheat swells more than wheat; but it is always difficult to get the exact proportions required by measurement; for different grades of flour require different proportions of water for the same thickness of batter; and I find that in all batter cakes and muffins raised with yeast it is better to stir them a little too thick than too thin; for just before baking they can be made thinner without injuring their quality; whereas, if you thicken by adding more flour, it destroys somewhat of their lightness."

"I think, Kate," observed Emeline, "there is one serious objection to your method of making buckwheat cakes. The average cook won't take the trouble to make gruel for her buckwheat cakes."

"I know," I replied, "that women hate to be painstaking about these things; and I have a friend, an admirable housekeeper, who insists that her buckwheat cakes are just as good as mine; and her method is much simpler. She sets her cakes to rise the first thing after breakfast, using only cold water, buckwheat flour, yeast, and a little salt.

"She sets them to rise on a table in the kitchen, or some moderately warm room, and next morning thins them with a little warm milk or water, adding a little soda if necessary. After first starting her cakes, she never adds fresh yeast, but uses the batter left; to which she adds flour and water enough for the next morning. In my cook-book, Emeline," I went on to say, "I mean to make very emphatic this idea: that however cooks may make buckwheat cakes, they must be careful to give them abundant time to thoroughly ferment and rise; for.I think a great many buckwheat cakes are baked before they have risen to their best estate."

"Kate, do you know how to make good corn-bread?" asked Emeline. "I am especially fond of it. But I am so heartily sick of 'Indian bread,' and 'Indian cakes,' as Northern and Eastern cooks persist in calling the wretched preparations of corn meal they manufacture, that I hope you will devote a chapter of your book to the consideration of corn-bread."

"Thank you, Emeline, for the suggestion. Corn-bread being a Southern institution or specialty, is very much neglected by Northern and Southern cooks; or, when made by them, is so 'doctored,' as a general rule, that a genuine lover of the article scarcely recognizes it in the vile mixture of grease, soda, eggs, milk, and sugar, thickened with poor corn meal ground so fine as to be destitute of character or sweetness. Southern corn is as much superior to that grown at the North, as a Hubbard squash is to a yellow pumpkin; but Southern corn, ground as fine as the meal that is generally used at the North, loses much of its excellence. Southern cooks undoubtedly excel in the art of making corn-bread of various kinds, among which the pone and hoe-cake used to take first rank. But since open fires, Dutch ovens, and bake-kettles, have been superseded by ranges and cooking-stoves, pone and hoe-cake have been superseded by 'dodgers,' and other varieties of corn-bread, baked upon the griddle, or in the oven, as convenience dictates. The pone, in the old time, was made of meal, warm water, yeast, and a little salt; and after becoming light by fermentation, was baked,— a large loaf, in a Dutch oven, for five or six hours. The hoe-cake was still more simple, being corn meal mixed with warm water and a little salt, into a stiff dough, fashioned by the hands into cakes an inch thick, and baked on a board, tilted before the fire, or, in the negro cabins, upon the hoe, which no doubt gave it the name. The dodger is a legitimate descendant of the hoe-cake, and I think deserves precedence in the corn-bread ranks. To make it, take a quart of corn meal, a teaspoonful of sugar, and a salt-spoonful of salt. Scald with boiling water, leaving the paste so thick that when moulded into cakes in the hand it retains its form, or if placed upon the griddle with a spoon, will remain heaped and not spread into thin cakes. Put a piece of butter, half the size of a pea, just where the dodger is to be placed on the griddle, and when melted, lay the cake upon it. In like manner fill the griddle. When brown, turn them over; but just before turning, place a small bit of butter on each cake, and when turned, press it gently in the centre to flatten the rounded surface, and bring the cake close to the griddle at the edges. These cakes should be an inch thick; and they require half an hour to bake. The heat must, of course, be moderate, and the cakes may be turned several times if necessary. After being turned on the griddle and browned on both sides, they can be transferred to a pan and a hot oven, to finish baking; or they can be baked altogether in a hot oven, if desirable. Although these dodgers are very good baked in this manner for only thirty or forty minutes, they are much better when baked a longer time. An hour's baking in a moderate oven gives them a crisp sweetness, quite irresistible to lovers of corn-bread; and when properly made and baked, they are such delicious breakfast-cakes that I do not wonder one accustomed to them, turns in disgust from the messes often presented under the name of corn-bread, in which grease and soda bear so prominent a part, that the stuff smells and tastes like soap.

"Corn-muffins are very fine, made in this way: To a quart of corn meal add an ounce of butter, a teaspoonful of sugar, and a salt-spoonful of salt. Scald with boiling water, pouring the water on slowly, and stirring the mixture until all the meal is moistened. When cool, add the yolks of three eggs, and beat well through the dough; then add cold, sweet milk, a small portion at a time, beating thoroughly, until the batter is of proper thickness. Beat the whites to a stiff froth, and add half at a time, alternating with a measure of baking-powder mixed with a small quantity of meal. Bake in muffin-rings, gem cups, or shallow pans, in a quick oven. Made a little thinner, this batter may be baked upon the griddle as thin griddle-cakes,—although the Southern griddle-cakes, or 'slappers,' as the colored people call them, are made in a somewhat different manner. I stood by Aunt Nancy, a colored woman, who made them deliciously, and saw just how she did it. She put a quart of meal in a bowl, and in the centre made a nest or hole, into which she dropped a lump of lard as large as a hickory nut, a pinch of salt, and a small teaspoonful of sugar. Then she poured boiling water on slowly, stirring the meal until all was moistened, when, pressing it compactly together in the bottom of the bowl, she 'lef'' it to swell, honey,' while she brought out the griddle and greaser, and got things ready for the baking. This done, she returned to the cakes, and having ascertained that the dough was not too warm, she broke into it three eggs, stirring them briskly, with a spoonful or two of cold milk, through the dough. From time to time she added cold milk in small quantities, continuing the stirring until the batter was quite thin, when she announced,—

"'Dem's done ready, now, miss.'"

"'But you've forgotten the soda, Aunt Nancy,'" I said.

"'Forgot de sody,' she repeated, with infinite disgust, 'what for should I go spile dem slappers with sody?'"

"In answer to my question why she didn't beat the eggs before she put them in the batter, she said emphatically, 'Better dis yere way, honey. You take my 'vice, and don't go trying' no 'speriments wid dese yere slappers.' I did, however, try the experiment of beating the eggs separately, after which I agreed with Aunt Nancy that they were better 'dis yere way.'

"This same 'slapper' batter, left a little stiffer, baked in the oven in shallow pans, cut in squares and served hot, is a very fine specimen of cornbread, sometimes called Cape May bread."

"Cousin Kate, do you know why the 'slappers' are better for having the eggs beaten only in and with the batter?"

"I think I do. But I don't mean to tell you, Alice, for the reason that I wish you to solve those riddles yourself, the reading of which requires only a little mild thinking."

"Speaking of riddles, reminds me of something," said Alice, "I intended mentioning to you half an hour ago. Have you or ma seen the absurd article in the 'Democrat'?"

"No," exclaimed both Emeline and myself, involuntarily.

"Then listen to this," was Alice's reply, as she unfolded the Westfield "Democrat," and read to us the following:—

"ABOUT GHOSTS.—For some weeks it has been the current report that ghostly visitants have taken possession of the Douglas mansion, which is in charge of the gardener during the absence of the family, and hold private seances there, on which occasions they materialize or assume the forms they wore while tarrying in this mundane sphere in years gone by. Although we have but little faith in either the ghosts or the reports, many of our readers appear to be deeply interested in both, and wish us to give them all the information that can be obtained upon the subject. We have therefore detailed a special reporter, in whom we have the utmost confidence, to work up the case, and give us the benefit of his investigations, and we hope shortly to lay before the readers of the 'Democrat,' a full account of the ghosts and their doings. Our reporter has been on duty several days, but has not as yet made much progress. The gardener, he says, 'doesn't interview worth a cent,' and he adds, very emphatically, 'the old fellow's wife is more secretive than a clam.' He is busily engaged reading up on the literature of 'spooks,' and hobgoblins generally, so as to be equal to the emergency, and fully prepared to tackle any sort of a ghost that may present itself. The facts he has gathered are very few and unsatisfactory, but we have high hopes of his giving us something racy in a short time, for he is willing to swear that he has had frequent glimpses of a creature, not of the earth earthy, flitting about the garden and veranda in the twilight, with hair floating about her shoulders, and dressed in the traditional white robes that ghosts are said to assume when they appear to mortal eyes."

CHAPTER VI.

BREAKFAST-TABLE GOSSIP.

"Kate, do I understand you to say that this coffee, which is so perfectly clear, has nothing used for settling it, but a spoonful of cold water?"

As I took the coffee she handed me, I answered, "At the time of making, nothing but water is added to the coffee; but at the time of browning, one egg is mixed with a pound of coffee. Coffee can be settled perfectly with a spoonful of cold water; but it stays settled better, and is not so easily disturbed or roiled, where egg is used. A cup of first-rate coffee, Emeline, is something rarely found on the average American table; nor is it surprising, perhaps, when we consider that making coffee is a delicate matter, and that the beverage is so easily spoiled, at any point from the beginning to the end of the process. Several things are requisite in order to have good coffee. First, the coffee must be of good quality, carefully picked over, and cleaned by rubbing in a dry towel. Next, it must be properly roasted. There are very perfect mechanisms for browning coffee; but any woman can roast it perfectly in the oven, if she attends to it. In a medium-sized dripping-pan a pound can be roasted at a time. The person roasting the coffee should give it her undivided attention while it is in the oven, otherwise she will often forget, and the coffee be spoiled. Coffee should roast slowly at first, an occasional shaking to change the position of the grains being all the attention it requires. After remaining ten or fifteen minutes in the oven, the heat may be increased, and the shaking must be done more frequently. Towards the last it must be looked at every few minutes, lest unawares it surprise you with too dark a browning. But how brown it should be, depends somewhat upon the taste of the drinker and the kind of coffee used. Rio will bear a browner tinge than Java. If the coffee, when made, is pale in color, and tastes of the bean,— that is, has a raw taste,— it is not sufficiently roasted. If it is black, and tastes bitter and burnt, it is overdone. It is a good plan to keep a spoonful of coffee unground, from one roasting till the next, in order to compare the newly roasted with it. When the coffee is roasted, pour it into an earthen dish to cool; and when so cool that you can clasp a handful of it tightly in your palm and feel it only warm — not hot — add to it a fresh egg, and with a fork stir it until perfectly mixed and each kernel has a share of the egg. The warmth of the coffee should be just sufficient to dry the egg adhering to it, and not cook it. When dry, the egg does not interfere with the grinding. Egg used in this manner is neither so troublesome nor expensive as when added at the time of making the coffee. Another convenient, inexpensive method is to wash eggs before breaking, and preserve the shells for settling coffee.

"The grinding of coffee is an important consideration. If ground very coarse, much of the strength remains in the grounds, some of which are often seen floating about in your cup, in an independent manner, and an isolated condition. If ground too fine, it will be muddy in spite of everything. Of course a happy medium is right. Some ladies have coffee prepared in one pot and poured into another before sending to table; but this is a bad practice, for every time coffee is exposed to the air it loses some of its aroma and excellence. When I have a fragrant perfume of coffee in my chamber while dressing, I take it for granted that I shall miss at breakfast the delicious aroma that has been so freely exhaled all over the house. If it is borne to me on the wings of the morning up three flights of stairs, how can I hope to find it concentrated in my cup at breakfast? Really excellent coffee can be made in various ways. The most perfect method of making it, perhaps, is by dripping the boiling water through the coffee.

But rare coffee may be made in the ordinary manner of steeping, if it is not allowed to boil enough to extract the bitter, or waste the aroma. There is one thing you must insist upon, Cousin Emeline, if you would have the best quality of coffee and tea; namely, *the pots must be kept clean on the inside.* If carefully washed every time they are used, they will not become dark and coated with deposits. Coffee made very strong, and diluted with boiled milk instead of water, is liked by many. That is a French style worthy of imitation. Mixed coffees are also considered by many finer in flavor than a single sort. I have tried various combinations, and like Rio and Java in equal proportions—or two parts Rio, two parts Java, and one part Mocha. To be most perfect, I think the different kinds should be roasted separately, and mixed afterward. But my advice to housekeepers is, experiment. Find out for yourselves what is best, and don't believe implicitly in any cook-book, not even Cousin Kate's. Use cook-books as helps, as hints, but not as infallible guides, and work out your salvation in cookery by the use of your own brains. A week's supply of coffee may be browned and ground at one time, if it is kept in air-tight cans or canisters.

"Most cooks use too little coffee. I allow a large tablespoon heaping full of ground coffee to a medium-sized cup and a half of water. Measure the coffee, and add to it a fresh egg, well beaten—unless egg has been mixed with it at the time of browning—and cold water enough to wet the whole. Beat it well together and, placing in the pot, add cold water till the pot is a third full. Set it where it will steep slowly, stirring it from time to time. Watch it closely, and as soon as it is about to boil, add more cold water. Keep adding cold water from time to time, just before the boiling takes place, until the pot is full. Then let it boil up once, settle, and serve."

"But supposing," said Alice, "that you didn't want a pot full of coffee, and that filling the pot would make it too weak, would you still fill the pot?"

"By no means," I replied. "But I would have the coffee-pot the size required, for you can't make a pint of coffee in a quart pot, and have it of perfect quality. If there is more room in the pot than is required, air fills the space and deteriorates the quality of the coffee. Beside, a pint of coffee tumbling about in a two-quart pot is sure to be unsettled in pouring. Alice, not long since I made coffee for a young gentleman, who, when asked if it was good, answered,—and his voice and face were very grave and serious,—'It is simply divine.'"

"O Cousin Kate!" laughingly exclaimed Alice; "I tremble when I think of the possible consequences of your having made such a cup of coffee, had that young man been twenty years older."

"Or Cousin Kate twenty years younger," I rejoined. "But, nonsense aside, Alice, I'm sure you would like to know just how that coffee was made. It was mixed coffee — two parts Rio, two parts Java, and one part Mocha, all of the best quality. In strength, it was made in the proportion of three heaping table-spoonfuls of coffee to one and a half cups of water. That, you see, is three times as strong as the directions just given. It was made with cold water, carefully steeped, and perfectly settled, and, before pouring, the cup was two-thirds filled with boiled milk, and then filled with the strong coffee; which made, in the estimation of that young man, a 'draught fit for the gods.'

"In boiling milk for coffee, Alice, do not let it actually boil, but let it come just as near boiling as possible and escape it, for it must be very hot. But the flavor is finer in coffee if it is taken after it is so heated as to be inflated with fine bubbles, but not actually boiled. With a milk-boiler this is easily managed; for, just at the right moment, it can be set back and kept hot for a long time."

While we were loitering over breakfast, discussing the merits of coffee, Tom, the gardener's son, brought us the morning mail. Among various and sundry letters, postal-cards, etc., I found the following missives, the first from an old bachelor cousin of mine, and the other from an intimate lady friend. The old bachelor, who is very abstemious in his habits, and exceedingly fond of English breakfast tea and dry toast, wrote :—

"When do you expect to find leisure for that long-promised cook-book? I do hope you will write it soon, and will give such minute directions in it for making both tea and toast, that no one can fail to understand them. Strange as it may seem, our best cook-books are ominously silent, or hopelessly bewildering, about the methods of making either; and I pray you to step to the front, and furnish the much-needed information. It would appear, at first blush, as if any one might make good tea or good toast without instruction; yet it is a singular fact, that at the average table one is about as great a rarity as the other. I confess to a weakness for 'the cup that cheers but does not inebriate,' for, to my taste, no other beverage is so delicious as well-made tea; but for the sloppy, bitter, or smoky-tasting decoctions that are foisted upon us at hotels, restaurants, and private houses, under that name, I have the most ineffable contempt. It is an insult to any decent stomach to force into it the wretched slops so barbarously extracted from the Chinese herb. I write feelingly on this subject, for it has been my privilege to drink tea properly made, and fragrant memories of the delicious flavor linger with me, effectually spoiling my relish for the common, vile decoction.

"As for dry toast, I dare say no woman would be willing to confess she did not know how to toast bread; yet my experience is, that good toast is the exception. Bad bread, scorched or burned, and sent to the table cold and tough, is as uninviting a dish as can be served; while a plate of crisp, hot toast, properly prepared, is more appetizing and tempting to the average man than the dantiest of hot cakes or muffins. Give me a cup of nice coffee or tea, with a plate of crisp, richly-browned toast, and firm, golden butter, for my morning or evening meal, and I will be content with *any* relish you choose to add—even chipped beef; or I will be satisfied with tea and toast alone, if both are at their level best.

"Do make haste and enlighten the world about tea and toast. For so doing, you will deserve its everlasting gratitude, and shall have, at least, that of Cousin John."

"Poor John! it is too bad that a folorn old bachelor can't have the small comfort to be found in tea and toast," observed Emeline, as I finished reading the letter. "I hope you will comply with his requests. Your toast is always perfection itself, and I think even Cousin John would be quite satisfied with the English breakfast tea you give us here, Kate; for I never drank finer, even in England. How long do you boil it, and how do you manage always to have it just right?"

"I do not boil it at all. And following precisely the same method of making every time, why should the quality of the tea vary? I think it would be safer for a careless, inattentive cook to boil the tea, if it did not boil more than a minute, for to make it without boiling, three requisites must be faithfully observed. The pot must be as hot, when the tea is put into it, as boiling water can make it. The water must be boiling when poured upon the tea, and the tea must stand, before being poured, from five to ten minutes. This is the recipe I shall give for making English breakfast tea: Ten or fifteen minutes before making the tea, fill the teapot with boiling water, and the tea-kettle with cold water, freshly drawn. It makes a vast difference with the quality of the tea whether it is made of water freshly boiled or of stale water that has stood in the kettle and been re-boiled, until all the sparkle and life have gone out of it. As soon as the kettle boils, empty the tea-pot, rinsing it with boiling water. Put into it a heaping teaspoonful of tea to each person, allowing a cup and a half of water to the same. Cover closely, letting it stand from five to ten minutes before pouring. Cream is as essential to good tea as it is to good coffee; and in both cases is best when the hot liquid is poured upon it. When all the tea is poured from the pot, boiling water may be added to extract the remaining strength from the leaves."

"I suppose," said Emeline, "you make green tea somewhat different? Isn't it a general rule to boil black, and to steep green teas?"

"I believe so. But my practice is, when trying a new kind or grade of tea, to experiment by various methods of making, and ascertain which method is best for the particular kind of tea. As a general rule I find all black and English breakfast teas of finest flavor, when made after the manner I have just given. Occasionally I find a sort that is better boiled for two or three minutes; but I have never discovered any that was improved by being boiled and stewed indefinitely. I think all green teas best, steeped in a small quantity of water ten or fifteen minutes — the bulk of the water being added just before the tea is poured. Mandarin tea, of which I am very fond, is much better steeped for fifteen minutes with only a small quantity of water. This tea, which is only sold by the Woman's Tea Company, has a peculiar flavor, decidedly individual, and not likely to be mistaken for a common herb; and those who make it properly soon grow to like it very much."

"Do you use the same quantity of tea to the same amount of water in all cases?" asked Alice.

"By no means," I replied. "The quantity of tea required depends upon the strength of the tea, and the taste of the drinker. A greater bulk is required of coarse, than of fine tea; and both coarse and fine teas vary much in strength. In making tea, as in most things relating to cookery, good sense and discriminating care are essential on the part of the cook.

"To make the meanest toast possible take bread that is a little sour, a trifle raw, or not quite light, and is not fit to eat untoasted. Lay it on a gridiron over a hot fire, where it will burn before it even dries. When burned sufficiently to taste bitter, spread it with strong butter and pack the slices one above the other, allowing it to become cool before serving, and you have a dish that would ruin the digestion of an ostrich, and that no sensible person should touch. The woman who thinks good toast can be made of bad bread labors under a terrible delusion. Most of the attempts to improve bad bread or bad butter prove futile, as no amount of doctoring can change their normal condition. They generally retain all their original badness in spite of their disguises and conversions. To make the best quality of toast, the bread must be good. If stale, it will toast quickly by being held a short distance from a clear fire. If fresh, lay the slices on a grate, or wire frame, in a hot oven until slightly dried. A toasting-fork is much better for toasting bread than a gridiron, as, held by a fork, the entire surface of the bread is exposed to the clear fire, and the distance between the toast and the fire can be increased or lessened at will. Serve toast hot in a toast-holder, or laid singly on a plate. If the slices are piled one upon another they sweat and become tough and clammy. Most persons prefer to butter toast for themselves, and many dislike it soaked with melted butter."

The letter from my lady friend Fanny, ran thus:

"I hope you are making some progress in your efforts to ameliorate the unhappy condition of the people who eat. Unfortunately, I'm in a position to appreciate the need of your labors, for, alas! I'm boarding. For dinner to-day we had spring lamb and green pease, the first of the season, and both were unfit to eat by reason of being underdone—that is, raw. After tasting the pease, I shoved them away in disgust, and with an injured feeling which I think not conducive to digestion, I picked out bits of lamb so far cooked that the squeaking sound it made while undergoing friction from my teeth, in a very faint degree resembled the far-off bleating of a lamb; and that resemblance, I'm certain, was pure imagination, for I have no doubt the lamb was dead, even if it was not cooked. Had the pease been sufficiently boiled, they would still have been nearly worthless, as our cook belongs to that class of idiots who drain pease; deliberately pour away their life and sweetness, leaving for our nourishment only the dry husks. I hope in your book you will castigate such cooks severely. Another senseless practice is to boil pease in a bag, in a pot of water. The only advantage this method has is, that soup is sometimes made of the water—which is a very questionable one; for to eat soup in warm weather, in order to save the juice of the pease, is like the economy of taking medicine to prevent its being wasted. I doubt if *you* can give a better receipt for cooking green pease than this: To a quart of green pease add a half-pint of boiling water, cover closely, and simmer gently until very tender, at which time the water should be nearly evaporated. Season *lightly* with salt and pepper, adding a little butter, or sweet cream. I wish you to italicize that word *lightly*, for most cooks ruin pease with salt. And please suggest good taste requires that pease should be moist enough to necessitate being served at table in sauce-dishes, and eaten with a spoon. I detest pease so hard and dry that they roll and tumble about my plate, when I make vain efforts to entice them on my fork, and I usually soon abandon the fruitless chase. And, Kate, don't forget the claims of asparagus. For, next to pease, I think it suffers most at the hands of stupid cooks. I have seen it served in all the intermediate stages between asparagus soup and asparagus mush; and have known it to be mixed with dandelions, mustard, and lamb's quarter. In rinsing, it is not enough to pour water over the asparagus. Each stalk should be held separately by the base, and swashed back and forth in a large pan of water until free from sand and dust. Then it should be tied in small bunches, and laid carefully in a stewpan of boiling water, slightly salted. Let the water barely cover the vegetable. Simmer gently until very tender and perfectly cooked. Have ready a platter, covered with small slices of dry toast. With a fork lift a bunch of asparagus by means of the string around it, let it drip for an instant, then place it carefully upon a slice of toast. When all is so placed, cut and remove the strings. Pour over it drawn butter made with milk, or simply melted butter. The toast is not only a palatable accompaniment, but is useful in serving the vegetable."

"I was reading the other day," said Alice, "about the etiquette of high-toned society in New York. Among other things, I learned that it is there considered vulgar to eat the toast upon which the asparagus is served."

"I know of no better method of cooking pease or asparagus than those described by Fanny, and shall certainly preserve her letter among my cook-book scraps. String beans and green lima beans should be cooked in the same manner as green pease. Dried beans, a palatable, nutritious vegetable, are seldom seen upon our tables, save as the old, time-honored, traditional baked pork and beans, a dish which the average modern stomach rejects as too strong. But why discard the bean because pork and beans make too hearty a dish, or because the discovery of trichina has spoiled our relish for pork? To cook dried beans, place them on the back of the stove in a plentiful supply of cold water. When swelled, drain the water off and give them a fresh supply. Let them simmer until parboiled. Drain again, adding enough hot water to finish cooking. Boil gently till soft, and, when done, season with salt, pepper, and butter. Serve them at this stage as stewed beans; or, place them in a deep dish, and bake in a hot oven, and you have baked beans, without the addition of pork. Care should be taken to always have beans thoroughly cooked, as otherwise they are indigestible and unwholesome."

"Kate," said Emeline, "I can give you a better method for baking beans. Pick and soak the beans over night in cold water. In the morning put them into fresh cold water to boil, and simmer gently till the skins break, and they seem about to fall to pieces. Then season to taste with salt, pepper, and butter; or, use pork, if preferred, adding a tablespoonful of molasses to every two quarts of beans. Put the beans in a deep crock, place them in a moderate oven, and let them bake indefinitely, only it must be a long indefinitely. Add water from time to time, if necessary, to keep them from becoming too dry. When they assume a reddish-brown tinge, something akin in color to Boston brown bread, their perfect state is approaching; and they can be put into a baking-dish, suitable to send to the table, and nicely browned in the oven; or they can be set aside until next day and re-baked in time for dinner. Now, Kate, if you can place beside this recipe one for Boston brown bread, your cook-book will be appreciated. By the way, I wonder if this admixture of molasses in baked beans gave rise to the assertion that Yankees eat pork and molasses."

"Are we," asked Alice, "to understand that green vegetables are to be put to cook in hot water, and dried ones in cold water?"

"All dried vegetables should certainly be put into cold, or lukewarm, water; but there is a difference of opinion in regard to fresh vegetables. Some cooks contend that it preserves their green color to put them into boiling water, but as I fail to see why vegetables are more desirable on account of shades of colors, that suggestion has no weight with me. From experiments that I have made, I fail to discover any material difference between putting green vegetables to cook in cold, warm, or boiling water; consequently, I use whichever is most convenient."

"Cousin Kate," observed Alice, "as my favorite vegetable is sweet corn, I should like to know your pet method of cooking it."

"I prefer it stewed," I said, "as it retains all its sweetness when cooked in that manner. Cut the corn from the cob; but be careful, in so doing, not to cut any portions of the cob. Scrape off the milk, also the eyes of the grains. When you have prepared all your corn, put it in a stew-pan, adding not more than half a pint of water to a quart of corn. Cover closely and stew gently for thirty or forty minutes, stirring frequently at first to prevent it sticking to the kettle and burning. By the time it is thoroughly cooked the water will have evaporated, and you can season to taste with salt and butter; or you can use sweet cream, if you prefer it to butter. Corn cooked in this way is much sweeter than when steamed or boiled, and it is much easier to cut it from the cob before than after it is cooked.

"Corn oysters I think especially nice. They are made in this manner: Split each row of kernels through the middle, while on the cob. Shave off thinly, then again in the same way, and finally scrape off the eyes and milk. This method of preparing the corn is much nicer than grating it. To the corn from eight or ten medium-sized ears, add the whites of three eggs, beaten to a stiff froth, and three tablespoonfuls of flour. Add the egg and flour alternately, first egg and then flour, in two or three portions, stirring them in with a fork. Season lightly with salt and pepper, and fry the same as oysters, putting a spoonful at a time on the griddle, or in the spider. Fry in a small quantity of lard and butter mixed. Brown on both sides and serve on a heated platter."

"Kate, *I* beseech you," Emeline said, as soon as I paused, "that you deal justly with the potato —the white potato that we eat at all meals, and in all seasons, nearly every day of our lives. What a sorry, sad-looking object it is as it comes from the hands of some cooks, sent to the table in its dingy jacket, or sallow and waxen, without its jacket, that having been hastily removed just before serving. But served in either of these styles it is preferable to that miserable mash, bluish in color, full of lumps and cold stiffness, or watery and rank in flavor."

"Your descriptions," I replied, "are perfect, Emeline; I recognize each as an old acquaintance. The white, or Irish potato, when full grown, I think, is always better pared before cooking. Not only pared, but well pared. Having carefully removed all the dark eyes and dingy spots, let the potatoes lie for an hour or two in a plentiful supply of cold water, and then put them to boil, in a large quantity of boiling water. They should boil moderately, and as soon as tender at the heart, be drained, partly covered and set to dry on the back of the stove. Every minute or two give them a gentle shake, so that they roll over and change positions, until they are perfect snowballs of powdery whiteness. If served in this state, you will find them the perfection of boiled potatoes. I think very few would pass them by untasted. If mashed, the potato should be made fine and free from all lumps, before cream, milk, or butter is added. After the seasoning is in, beat well with a wooden spoon, or potato-beater, until light. Serve hot.

"This is a general rule for boiling potatoes; but like all rules it has exceptions. Different varieties of the vegetable require different methods of cooking. Some may be better placed to boil in cold water and allowed to heat gradually, as the water heats; others in a small quantity of water; while others — the peach-blow, for instance — should never be boiled at all, but should be either baked or steamed. When baked in a hot oven, the peach-blow is dry, mealy, and white, and always satisfactory. It is also the same steamed. But boiled, it is worse than a disappointment. It is a hard-hearted thing with all its tenderness on the surface; and boil it as you will, the result is unsatisfactory

—usually hardness at the core, while the outside is cooked into a mush or gruel. To drain and dry properly under these circumstances is difficult. But no woman should rest content with an imperfect dish of potatoes. If one method of cooking fails she should try another.

"An agreeable companion to fried chicken is fried potato, done in this way: Slice very thin, soak for an hour or two in cold water, changing the water once or twice. Drain the slices in a strainer, and dry them on towels, by rolling and tumbling them from one towel to another. Have the slices separate, not packed together, when put into the boiling lard. Fry the same as chicken. When of a light brown, lift, by means of a wire skimmer — an indispensable thing in every well-ordered kitchen — and drain in a wire or tin sieve. Serve hot. The last water in which the slices lie may be slightly salted, or a very slight sprinkling of salt given them when served.

"Stewed potato, a nice breakfast dish, is easily prepared. Cut the potato in slices about an eighth of an inch in thickness. Boil gently until tender, but not quite done. Drain the water away, adding sweet cream and seasoning. Cover closely and stew very gently for a few minutes. A little minced parsley, if liked, may be added.

"Browned potatoes are very nice for dinner, with

a roast. Pare and place them in the dripping-pan around the meat. Turn them over when partly done, that they may brown evenly. Potatoes of medium size require an hour to cook in this manner."

CHAPTER VII.

AT DINNER.

"I THINK, Cousin Emeline, there is no dish more usually detestable in America than soup. Were I to describe most truthfully what I have usually found passing under that name, I should call it greasy water, well seasoned with pepper and salt, and having in it macaroni, rice, or stringy bits of vegetables,— a mixture both unwholesome and unpalatable. In my cook-book I mean to insist that one of the cardinal virtues of good cooking is, that food shall be so prepared as not to taste watery. I have often dined where every article of food upon the table could have been properly labelled 'watery,' for the soup was watery, the roast was watery, the vegetables were watery, and even the pies and puddings were watery. But this soup which Alice has served us to-day, would silence the complaints of the most inveterate grumbler. It is lovely to look at, being of a rich color, between amber and ruby, and the flavor is like a mingling of many good things, whereby something far better has been produced, than is concealed in any single ingredient. You taste neither water, meat, vegetables, herbs, nor spices. You cannot be sure this, that, or the other went to make up the delicious whole. You relish it. It is appetizing, satisfying, and worthy of being called soup. The cook who serves a soup like this is an artist, with fine tastes and keen perceptions; and although neither Alice nor I could give the exact recipe, the general rules for making soup are easily laid down, and each cook must put in the delicate finishing touches according to taste and fancy.

"In the first place a soup-kettle must be a soup-kettle, and nothing else. And unless made with a false bottom it should stand on a rest that raises it from the stove, so that its contents shall not be in danger of burning. Let the cover fit closely. Put into it a beef bone, carefully washed and broken; the trimmings of beefsteak, veal cutlets, lamb chops; the refuse pieces of cold meat of all sorts, roasted, boiled or fried; also game, fresh fish, the skeletons of roast chicken or turkey, beefsteak bones, and all scraps that are good for nothing else,—bearing in mind always that they must be cleaned and not burned. Never allow the soup-kettle to boil, but let it simmer unceasingly. When all the desirable qualities are extracted from the bones and meat by this long-continued simmering, strain the contents of the kettle into an earthen bowl. Cover, and set aside.

In cold weather, soup 'stock,' as this preparation is called, may be kept for many days, especially if the surface covering of grease is not removed; but in warm weather it should only be kept, and then in a cool place, from one day until the next. Before returning the stock to the soup-kettle, carefully remove all the grease, and add barley, rice, macaroni, vermicelli, vegetables, or such ingredients as desired, according to the sort of soup to be made. The carrot I consider one of the most important vegetables for soup, as it has a good taste and a rich color, and is wholesome. Tomatoes and onions come next in order; but the latter should be used only for flavoring, and sparingly. The soup which has inspired my observations was, I think, made in this manner: To two quarts of soup stock, two carrots, ten tomatoes, one onion, and a pinch of thyme or sweet marjoram were added. When the vegetables were simmered to pieces, the soup was strained, the shreds of vegetables thrown away, and the soup returned to the kettle. A tablespoonful of flour, stirred to a smooth paste with a little butter, was added when the soup came to a boil, also a little salt and pepper. Care was taken not to overdo the seasoning, but to blend everything perfectly. And just before serving, Alice put into the soup-tureen diced toast; that is, dry toast, very crisp, cut in small square bits. These bits of toast are best when added to the soup by the hostess just before serving, as then they reach the mouth in a dry, or less soaked condition, and, requiring some mastication, assist the digestion of the soup. Instead of toast, bread may be cut into small bits and fried in butter, until brown and crisp, or carrots cut in the same form and stewed until tender, may be added in place of either, or the soup may be served clear. When carrots, tomatoes, and browned bits of meat and bones are not used in preparing soup, a tablespoonful each of flour, butter, and sugar, browned together and added to the soup, gives it a rich color and fine flavor. Pure broths of beef, mutton, or chicken, delicately seasoned with salt and pepper, and having no other ingredients than rice or barley, are always good, and in many respects better than more elaborate soups. But broths, as well as soups, should have their distinct flavors, and should not be mere sloppy or greasy gruel, ferociously salted and peppered.

"This leg of lamb, Alice, is done to a turn, which cannot truthfully be said of the average roast. Meat should be put to roast in as hot an oven as it will bear without burning. After the outside is browned and crusted over, imprisoning the juices within, the heat may be somewhat lessened. But I recommend roasting all meats as quickly as possible. The roast should be placed in the pan without water or drippings. When cooked, it may be sprinkled with salt and pepper, if desired. The practice, so much in vogue, of slopping water over meat to 'baste' it, is very objectionable. It brings out the juices, and toughens and injures the quality of the meat. Salt, for the same reasons, should not be sprinkled over the meat before, or while, roasting. Veal is an exception to the general rule. Being a dry, tasteless meat, I think it is improved by frequent bastings with a well-seasoned gravy, to which a piece of butter and a teaspoonful of sugar have been added. Veal should be cooked more thoroughly than any other kind of meat except pork, —in fact should be cooked to death. Roast veal is best when cold.

"A roast of beef is much improved by searing the cut sides just before putting it in the oven. This is done by laying it in a hot pan or spider, over a bright fire, for two or three minutes. As soon as one side is brown, turn it over in the spider and brown the other, and place in a hot oven immediately. In roasting meat it is customary to allow fifteen minutes to each pound of beef, and twenty-five minutes to each pound of lamb or mutton. But when it has been seared before it is placed in the oven, at least half an hour can be deducted from the usual time allowed an ordinary roast of eight pounds. The advantage of the searing process is not, however, so much in saving time in roasting, as in saving the juices of the meat by the instant forming of crusts on the outside. I feel confident that no sensible woman, after a fair trial of the method of roasting meats by placing them dry in the pan, will ever return to the old way of basting them with water or drippings. It is a prevalent idea that meat will burn in roasting, if not basted, or wet with drippings; but the fact is, meat will bear all the heat necessary to roast it in the most perfect manner, and not burn. Resting dry upon the bottom of the pan, upper and under sides brown evenly at the same time; and not only is the process of roasting shortened, but nearly all the trouble of changing the positions of the meat in the oven is avoided.

"To boil meats or fowls, put them in boiling water and simmer smartly, until tender. Never allow them to boil fast or furiously, as so doing toughens the meat, and at the same time robs it of its juices. The smallest quantity of water possible should be used in boiling meats, and no salt should be added until the meat is nearly done. The fowl or joint should be covered closely, and frequently turned in the pot while boiling. Ham is best put in cold water and simmered gently until well done. The ham should be placed in the boiler with the skin down, and with sufficient water to cover it. After it begins to boil, fifteen minutes to each pound it weighs is not too much time to give it for thorough boiling. When removed from the water it should be allowed to cool before it is skinned. After skinning, place it in a pan, cover the outside thickly with white sugar, saturate with wine or vinegar, and brown richly in a moderate oven. Smoked ham should always be soaked over night in cold water, scraped and well washed before boiling.

"Salted meats, such as corned beef, tongue, etc., if too salt to be boiled in a small quantity of water, should be soaked in cold water, which extracts the salt without injuring the meat."

"Kate, in your cook-book do you mean to consider the whole bill of fare from beginning to end; or will you select from it here and there, taking only such articles and subjects as seem to you most needing consideration?"

"To discuss, or even glance at our whole bill of fare would require more time than I could give were I to live to threescore and ten. All I hope to do is to call attention to the importance of the subject, and to suggest such improvements in methods of cooking as have come under my personal observation. I shall not lumber up my cook-book with numberless untried recipes, but will endeavor to give the general principles that underlie them all; so that by its aid any woman with an ordinary quantity of brains will be enabled to prepare all kinds of food in a proper and healthful manner.

"How delicious these onions are, Alice,— tender and sweet, without being overdone into a tasteless mush. I seldom find beets, onions, or cabbage cooked to my liking. Beets are usually underdone, while onions and cabbage are overdone, and served with a supply of water quite unnecessary. Onions, cabbage, turnips, and all greens should be gently pressed in a colander until free from water; then placed in a heated dish, and seasoned with salt, pepper, and butter. Young dandelions and spinach are delicious so served."

"Kate, in France, I found a very nice dinner-dish, which I wish you would put into your book. It has three recommendations: It is palatable, ornamental, and inexpensive. Take a piece of beef, where lean and fat are mixed,— a rib cut is nice, if not too fat; boil gently until very tender, in well salted water. Make tomato sauce by stewing tomatoes and straining out the seeds. Place the tomatoes in a saucepan over the fire and season with butter, salt, pepper, and a little sugar; lastly, add a spoonful of arrowroot or corn-starch, wet with water. Boil. The tomato sauce should be of the consistence of thick gravy, and perfectly smooth. Serve, by placing the meat on a hot platter and pouring the sauce over it.

A beef tongue cooked and served the same way is delicious." And Emeline continued: "Kate, I incline to the opinion that enjoyment of a meal depends in great measure upon the suitability of the things composing it. One can, no doubt, acquire a taste for almost any kind of food; but while some kinds appear to be divorced by nature, other kinds seem to be designed expressly to go together."

"You are right," I replied. "White potatoes, for instance, are suitable with nearly everything. Baked potatoes are universally acceptable with cold meats for dinner; and with beefsteak, chops, or picked-up codfish for breakfast. They are especially good with all kinds of fresh fish, and also with fried or scalloped oysters. Mashed or plain boiled potatoes should be served with stewed chicken, and roast meats or fowls with which gravies are served. Sweet potatoes seem most at home with roast beef, lamb, and fowls. Turnips and cabbages are appropriate with mutton and corned beef. Onions with beefsteak, roast beef, and roast fowls. Tomatoes are good with fish, flesh, or fowl; but are especially good with fat meats or poultry. This is also the case with sour baked or stewed apples. Sour baked apples are also nice with hash, for breakfast.

"But the suitability of food is a fruitful theme, and should be as much a subject of study as the suitability of sounds or colors. The idea has somehow obtained that it is improper or undignified for intelligent men and women to make a study of gastronomy. The cultivated stomach, however, appreciates contrast and harmonies in taste as keenly as the cultivated eye or ear does in color or sound; and I am satisfied, in my own mind, that the stomach is as much jarred and disarranged by inharmonious tastes as either eye or ear by inharmonious sights or sounds. The stomach is the most important, as well as the most delicate, organ in a human being. It is not merely a receptacle for stuff that has tickled the palate, or for food that will sustain life. It is the workshop in which are prepared all the materials essential to the building up of body and brain, and its needs and demands should be treated with thoughtful consideration."

"Cousin Kate, don't forget our rice pudding," said Alice.

"Ah, no! Let me help your mother. See, as the spoon cuts through the light brown skin, a rich, creamy substance appears; not of a pure white, but with a faint tinge of salmon. Each grain of rice is perfect in form and of large size, as if expanded to its utmost capacity; yet so soft that the slightest pressure is sufficient to crush it. This pudding is made of milk, rice, and sugar. It contains no raisins, butter, or water. The proportions are these: Eight measures of new milk, one measure of rice, one measure of sugar. If desired, it may be flavored with lemon, vanilla, or nutmeg, and a small pinch of salt should be added. Place it on the range, where it will heat slowly. Stir occasionally while the rice is swelling, and when the milk is boiling hot, place the pudding in a moderate oven and bake for one hour, or until the rice is quite soft. Do not stir the pudding after placing it in the oven, but try to ascertain if the rice is done before removing it. Serve cold. This simple pudding, I think, nine persons out of ten would prefer to those messes and mixtures compounded of boiled rice, eggs, fruit, and butter, and served warm with sauce. Yet the average cook takes extra pains to make the expensive, indigestible dish, while this simple, wholesome, and delicious dish seems to be almost unknown. The error of supposing that nearly every kind of food is improved by the addition of butter seems to be as wide-spread as it is damaging and false. While some dishes are improved for most tastes, by the judicious use of good butter, a vastly greater number are spoiled by the injudicious use of bad butter. And here I wish to say emphatically, that I know of no judicious use to which bad butter can be applied by a housewife, except that of making it into soap. To put bad butter into pastry, puddings, and vegetables, does not make the butter good. It simply spoils the pastry, puddings, and vegetables. Many dishes are overdosed with sweet butter; while others in which it it is usually found are much better without it. American cooks have entirely too much faith in the virtue and potency of grease."

"In looking over the 'American Woman's Home' the other day," observed Alice, "I came across a paragraph on butter, that I presume you would endorse. I will read it to you: 'A matter for despair as regards bad butter is, that at the tables where it is used it stands sentinel at the door to bar your way to every other kind of food. You turn from your dreadful half slice of bread which fills your mouth with bitterness, to your beefsteak, which proves virulent with the same poison. You think to take refuge in vegetable diet, and find the butter in the string-beans, and polluting the innocence of early pease. It is in the corn, in the succotash, in the squash. The beets swim in it; the onions have it poured over them. Hungry and miserable, you think to solace yourself at dessert, but the cake is acrid and the pastry is cursed with the same plague.'"

"But to change the subject, Kate, have you noticed," interrogated Emeline, "on how few tables you find rice that is properly cooked?"

"Yes, I have noticed with sorrow the ignorance and stupidity exhibited in the preparation of so simple an article of food.

"There are several excellent methods of cooking rice. This is one of them: After the rice has been carefully picked and washed, add three measures of warm water to one measure of rice, and soak for an hour. Then cook it in the same water, by setting the dish containing it in a steamer, and steaming it for one hour. When put to steam add a small quantity of salt, and stir two or three times with a fork during the first fifteen minutes. Rice cooked in this manner will be white and dry, with each grain separate and distinct, yet soft and palatable. If desired, part of the water can be left out, and its equivalent in milk added, when the rice is nearly done cooking. One advantage of this method is, that rice can be boiled in a china bowl, or any vessel preferred.

"If you wish to cook rice quickly, I know of no better way than this: Put one measure of rice in five measures of boiling water. Cover closely and boil rapidly, twenty or twenty-five minutes, till tender. Drain, partly cover, and set fifteen minutes, where it will keep hot, and dry off."

Alice seemed to be growing restless and impatient about something; but she gave no expression to her feelings except by a quick, nervous tapping of the toe of her kid slipper upon the carpet, and by a frequent pushing back of the stray curls which rested against her cheek. At last she sprang up joyfully, exclaiming: "Oh, Susannah, what a deal of work you must have had to do this morning. Where shall we go first? Up stairs, down stairs, or to the lady's chamber?"

"I always do *her* room first, and the drawing-room last," replied Susannah, adding: "Will you come too, Miss Kate? and perhaps the Madam wouldn't object."

Upon this invitation we all followed her upstairs, and through the dimly-lighted passage, to the suite of rooms heretofore mentioned as having been occupied by the late Mrs. Douglas. The main room was large, airy, and well-lighted. Opening out of this were two smaller ones — a bed-chamber and a dressing-room. The walls were of a soft gray tint, and were hung with paintings, engravings, and chromos. The carpet had a gray ground, covered with vines of the trailing arbutus, so perfect that, as our feet pressed them, we almost expected the delicious fragrance of the crushed flowers to come stealing up from their mossy bed. Window draperies, easy-chairs, and lounges were of gray cretonne, relieved by glowing vines and bright blossoms. All the furniture was of rose-wood, massive and delicately carved. At the foot of the bed stood a small crib, the lace curtains of which were looped back with rose-colored ribbons. By the side of the crib Alice paused, and, with trembling voice, asked, "Did the baby die too?"

"O yes, Miss, before the mother. And it was the

shock that killed her, I've no manner of doubt," answered Susannah. "You see that she was just hanging, sort of even balance between life and death, when the nurse announced thoughtlessly that the child was dead. At that she gave a little cry, and stretched out her arms, begging for her baby; and from that time she sank rapidly, sobbing and sighing, until she breathed her last. Now, I think if her baby had lived, she wouldn't have died." Susannah paused a moment, wiped her eyes with the corner of her check apron, and continued: "These bureau drawers, Miss Alice, are packed full of the handsomest baby things you ever saw. There are heaps and heaps of gossamer flannels, tiny socks and dainty night-dresses, and other things, all tucked and puffed with lace. Poor, dear lamb, she used to sit there in the sunshine sewing and singing day after day — singing in a low sweet voice a warble of some sort, just fit for a lullaby. And more than once I said to her, 'Miss Helen, I wouldn't make so many of those little things. It isn't a good sign?" Then she would reply, with a blush, 'Why, I think it is a very good sign indeed, Susannah. But go away with your superstitions. I put no faith in signs and omens.' And I don't think she believed a word in any of the signs; but, bless her dear heart, they came true all the same. And I suppose it was all for the best. For it matters little to any of us whether we die to-day, or to-morrow, or in a few years. The end soon comes anyhow."

"Cousin Kate, what is this?" interrupted Alice, holding up a small, beautifully bound volume, on the back of which, in letters of gold, was the name —"Helen Douglas."

"That," I answered, "is a memorial — a tribute to the dead wife, written by the husband during the first weeks of his bereavement. It contains some beautiful things. Wouldn't you like to look it over at your leisure?"

"Indeed, I should," was the reply; and Alice tucked the book under her arm, hugging it closely to her side, as if she regarded it as a rare treasure, while we followed Susannah to the drawing-room.

No sooner were the windows opened, and the room filled with light and sunshine than Alice excitedly exclaimed:

"Mamma, look at those pictures—'My lord' and his mother. Cousin Kate, what does it all mean? Who are these people?"

"That," I answered, quietly, "is the portrait of my old school-mate Jennie Douglas, and this a very good likeness of her son Gerald; while *this* is an idealized but faithful picture of his wife. Wasn't she a beautiful woman?"

"She *is* beautiful," said Alice. "I can't bear to hear to hear you say she *was* beautiful, as if her life was ended. Had I known her, I could never think of her as dead, I am sure."

"Kate," asked Emeline, "did you suspect that our Switzerland acquaintances were your friends, the Douglases?"

"I did suspect, in fact was sure of their identity from your very accurate descriptions. Quite a romance, isn't it, Alice? And that *you* should have dreamed of this man the first night you slept under his roof, not knowing of his association with these scenes, seems to me a singular coincidence. But there is no accounting for dreams, or the strange happening of events. The most unlooked for, as well as most unwished for circumstances, sometimes turn our lives into a new channel, and, in after days, we see what we thought at the time a great calamity, was, after all, for our best good."

"Yes," said Emeline, reflectively, "this life seems a sad muddle. We go groping about in the dark, seeing strange shapes of evil, and stumbling over neglected graves, longing for light, and praying for mists and fogs to roll away; and sometimes catching glorious glimpses of the evil shapes changing to friendly faces, and the sad graves becoming mounds of bloom and greenness. But, Kate, we have been here more than a month, and you have not devoted one hour to my novel. Now, on the first rainy day, I shall expect you and Alice to come to my room and spend the entire morning in listening to portions of it. I want your opinion about so many things — even about deciding .upon a title for it. To name my first-born and only child, I found an easy matter compared with determining what to call this fledgling of my imagination. I think a title should be attractive, and at the same time give a hint, at least, of the contents of the book, don't you?"

"Yes, that is well enough in a novel. But in the case of my cook-book I have a different opinion. That I intend to slip into libraries and on centre-tables, as well as into kitchens, and have it read by thousands, who would otherwise never look at it, by selecting a title that suggests pleasant light reading rather than a dry dissertation upon cookery. Won't I steal a march upon many an unsuspecting damsel, and teach hundreds how to cook before they realize they are reading a cook-book?"

"I never saw a more spiritual face," said Alice, still wrapt in contemplation of the portrait of Helen Douglas. As represented by the artist, she appeared a blonde with delicate features, whose large eyes and full mouth might have had in them a hint of voluptuousness, but for the pure, Madonna-like expression of the whole face. A flowing robe of fleecy white added to the effect.

Her hands were folded upon her bosom, one of them touching a large cross suspended from her neck by a tiny gold chain. This was the only ornament she wore. Her eyes were raised as if in prayer, and her light, wavy hair floated unconfined over her neck and shoulders.

"It is, indeed, very lovely, and it will be a wicked shame if the second Mrs. Douglas banishes it to the attic," was Emeline's response to her daughter.

A slight flush appeared on Alice's cheek, as she replied, "Mamma, Gerald Douglas looks to me like a man who, loving once, would love forever; but perhaps I can judge better what manner of man he is, after reading this memorial." And Alice left us, to peruse in her own room, the small gilt-edged volume dedicated to the memory of Helen Douglas.

CHAPTER VIII.

OMELET AND DAINTY DISHES.

"Broiled chicken for breakfast — how nice!" said Cousin Emeline, as she lifted the cover from the dish before me. "What a pity so few cooks can broil well! I've had more difficulty in the broiling department than in any other."

"Broiling, Emeline, when properly done, is a very satisfying method of cooking steaks, chops, chicken, etc., — satisfying to the eater thereof, I mean. But the poor housewife who broils herself as well as her meats, in the laborious effort to attain perfection, does not perhaps enjoy it to the same extent. With a suitable fire and other conveniences, broiling is not at all difficult. But with the average range or cooking-stove it is no easy matter, as the fire is seldom in right condition at the important moment. And my recommendation to women who toil and suffer to bring the broiled steak or chop to the table in perfection, is to try this method: At the time of placing the steak over the fire, put into the oven a dripping-pan large enough to hold the steak without folding. As soon as the steak is lightly browned on one side, turn and brown it on the other; then transfer it instantly to the hot pan and oven, where, if it be thick, it will need to remain from five to ten minutes, according to the state in which it is to be served. Serve on a heated platter, and season after removing from the oven. This method relieves the cook, saves all the juices of the meat, and prevents it from burning on the outside while it remains raw within. No one can tell a steak so cooked from one finished on the gridiron; and those who have tried both methods, find the hot-oven finish far superior. But it will not answer to have the oven warm merely. It must be hot. Or, steaks, chops, etc., may be broiled — literally broiled — in this way: Set your spider on the stove, and let it get smoking hot. Put in no butter nor any kind of grease. Have your meat previously prepared by trimming off all pieces of bone, gland, superfluous suet, and tissue that will bind the edge and make it turn up. Lay it carefully and smoothly in the spider. It will stick fast at first, but as soon as browned it can be loosened with a knife. When juice begins to appear turn it over, and let the other side brown the same as the first. Press closely to the pan when turned, and turn as often as is necessary to save the juices and cook the steak properly.

"Lamb or mutton chops are very nice, dipped in beaten egg, covered with bread-crumbs rolled fine, and fried like chicken, in a quantity of boiling lard. When broiled, they should always be done, like steak, in a hot pan, unless they are very much trimmed; that is, unless the small piece of lean tenderloin is separated entirely from the bone and fat, which should be rejected. These trimmed chops may be broiled over a clear fire in a wire gridiron, such as is used for oysters; and, when so cooked, are delicious. The rejected bone and fat can be saved in a stew, or in the soup-kettle. But it would be no more wasteful to throw them away, than to retain and broil altogether, as is usually done. For in the latter case the result is generally a badly damaged chop, smoked and burned from the dripping of grease — an unsightly, awkward piece, from which nine persons out of ten select and eat the small bit only, leaving the rest upon their plates to be thrown out with the scraps from the table. But in my cook-book, in connection with this recipe for broiling, I intend to put in staring capitals, KEEP THE BROILING-PAN PIPING HOT ALL THE TIME THE MEAT IS COOKING."

"Your labor-saving expedients," remarked Emeline, "may do well enough with chops and steaks, and may probably prevent them from being burned or underdone. But by no substitute for the gridiron, or by no make-believe method of the sort you recommend, could a broiled chicken be produced that would begin to approach this in excellence."

"Ah, ha!" said Alice, gayly, "you are in error there. This chicken has never touched a gridiron, nor seen live coals. It was done entirely in a hot oven, after one of Cousin Kate's labor-saving methods. This is the way it was cooked: The chicken was prepared for broiling by being opened down the back, washed in cold water, and wiped dry with a soft cloth. The breast-bone was flattened with a mallet, the wings were twisted back, to leave the breast exposed, and the chicken was placed, skin up, in a dripping-pan, and pressed close to the pan, to make it lie as flat as possible. After being thus fixed, I put it into a hot oven and shut the door. In about five minutes I heard a sputtering inside, and began to think something was wrong; but Cousin Kate dissipated my fears by assuring me that it was cooking nicely. From time to time I peeped into the oven, just to see that it was not burning, and at the expiration of twenty or twenty-five minutes I placed the chicken on a heated platter, seasoned it with pepper, salt, and butter, and here it is before us."

"Incomparable as a broiled chicken!" was Emeline's response.

"So thinks my fastidious mamma? But would you have thought so had you known before you tasted it that it was oven-cooked?"

"I do not think my prejudice in favor of broiling could prevent my appreciating so perfectly cooked a chicken as you have served us this morning, Alice. But why do you not season, and baste it with butter, before you put it in the oven? I would do so; and would also put water in the pan, to keep it from burning."

"There you would make a great mistake," said Alice, decidedly. "The pan must be dry, so that the chicken will brown on the bottom; and the chicken must be dry, so it may broil, instead of steam and stew. Besides, if the chicken was basted with butter it would brown with less heat; and Cousin Kate says the secret of success in this method, is in having the oven just as hot as the chicken will bear without burning. It would by no means be the same, in appearance or taste, if done in a slow, or even a moderate oven."

"All birds that are good broiled, are better when cooked in a hot oven in the manner Alice has just described," I remarked; when the appearance of Tom with the mail interrupted the conversation. Among my letters was one from my friend Mrs. Rose, containing some hints for my cook-book. In regard to quail, she wrote:

"'I think there is no bird more delicate than a quail broiled in this manner: Lay the bird on a gridiron, and, when it begins to brown, dip it into butter, seasoned with salt and pepper. Continue to broil and dip, until it is done brown — a nice yellow brown all over. Serve hot.'"

"You don't approve of that, Kate, do you?" interrupted Emeline; "it seems to clash with some of your theories."

"At all events, Emeline, I shall not condemn without trying it. And perhaps the use of the butter here to hasten the browning, may be a good thing, as otherwise the bird might be too much done before it was properly browned. But to return to the letter.

"'Wild ducks should be cooked as soon as possible after they are shot. I know that large quantities are sent to gentlemen in London, by their friends in this country. But by the time they reach them, I doubt not the English gentry think very much as Mrs. M. did, especially if their ducks are cooked in the same manner hers were. Her husband's brother sent her from Washington a pair of canvas-backs for which he paid $10; but she didn't think them as good as a pair of tame ducks she could buy in her own town for ten shillings. I asked her how she cooked them. She said she stuffed them with bread dressing, seasoned with onion, and baked them an hour and a half. Now this is my recipe: Draw out the entrails, and rinse the ducks; but don't soak them, as some ignorant cooks do, or you will lose the juices. Rub inside with salt and pepper, and put in each duck a piece of butter the size of an egg, and a teaspoonful of red wine. Roast twenty or twenty-five minutes. By no means allow the birds to be moved while roasting, lest their juices be spilled. When done they will be full of a bright red gravy. Remove carefully to, and serve on, a hot dish.

"'Terrapin gladdens the heart of an epicure, when prepared according to this recipe: Put the terrapins in a pot of boiling water. Let them boil gently two hours, or until you can pick off the skin with ease. Then lift from the water, take off the under shell, pick the skin from the feet, and remove the gall and sand-bag, and, if you choose, the entrails. Pick the meat from the bones. Cut in small pieces. Mash the eggs and livers in the water that runs from the terrapin while picking it up, and mix with the meat. Place in a stew-pan or chafing-dish, season to taste with butter, salt, pepper, and Madeira wine, and stew for a few minutes — just long enough to heat thoroughly. About an ounce of butter and a wine-glass of wine to a pint of prepared meat are the proper proportions.'"

"I presume Mrs. Rose's recipes are excellent, as she lived several years on the eastern shore of Maryland, where they are famous for serving such epicurean luxuries as canvas-back and terrapin, in the most approved manner. But let us get on with the letter: 'I hope you will devote a chapter in your book to omelets. Did I ever tell you, it took me seven years to learn how to make an omelet? Now, I don't mean you to understand that I devoted my undivided time and attention to the study of omelets alone, during that period; but as occasion offered, during seven years, I tried various and varying recipes from at least a score of cook-books. As directed, I beat the eggs together at one time, and beat them separately at another time. I put cream in some, and in some I minced ham, parsley, or onion. I made omelets as light as a puff and dry as a husk. I produced omelets soft and frothy, as well as omelets flabby and leathery. I concocted omelets that were certainly first cousin to scrambled eggs; and omelets more nearly related still to baked custard. But the omelet I was striving for,— the omelet I had found in my girlhood days at first-class hotels, and tables where I could not take the cook aside and ask how it was made,— this ideal omelet was not to be evolved from all the materials prescribed by these cook-books. Discouraged and disappointed I rested from my labors; and Harry and I ate eggs boiled, poached, and scrambled. But at last I obtained the object of my endeavors. One morning I found upon the table of an intimate friend *my omelet*. "Did you make this?" I asked, eagerly. "Tell me exactly how you did it. Begin at the beginning, and let me know every twist and turn of the process." "Why," she answered, with a complaisant smile, "it's the easiest thing in the world. For my family I take five eggs. I break them into a bowl, and beat them with a spoon, lightly, until I can dip up a spoonful. I beat them only enough to break them up, and render them manageable. I have ready a little minced parsley, salt, and pepper. I place my omelet-pan, which is never used for any other purpose, with an ounce of sweet butter in it, on the stove; and as soon as the butter is hot,— be careful not to let it brown,— I pour the omelet, rinse the egg from the bowl with three teaspoonfuls of sweet milk — cream is better — and pour it over the omelet in the pan. I then sprinkle in salt, pepper, and minced parsley, and set it to cook where it will have moderate heat. While cooking I stir it gently with a fork, and when almost done, place it for a moment where the heat is a little quicker, so it may brown lightly on the bottom. When ready to serve, I slip a knife-blade under one side, holding the pan slightly tipped, and fold the omelet over, leaving half the pan naked, and the omelet in the shape of a turnover pie. And now comes the only difficult part of the operation — that of turning the omelet from the pan upon the platter. Don't forget to heat the platter,— a cold omelet isn't fit to eat. Hold the pan close to, and partly over it. Give it a sudden dip — the pan, I mean — and a gentle flop, and there lies your omelet, just where you desired, — a neatly shaped, plump little thing, about three inches thick, moist, light, and, in my judgment, the best omelet that can be made."

"'I went home happy, intending to surprise Harry next morning with my ideal omelet — the dainty dish he had heard me talk about, and sigh for so often. But, alas, for human expectations! I made the omelet, and hesitated not until the time to stir it came. Then a score of perplexing questions arose. "Stir gently two or three times," was what my friend had said. But what *is* stirring gently? Does to stir gently mean to stir slowly? And how soon should I begin to stir? And why stir with a fork? As no one was present to answer these and the other questions that suggested themselves, I seized a fork and began stirring slowly, round and round. But the tines of the fork scratched over the bottom of the spider, and that seemed the only result of my labor. After waiting awhile, I stirred again. This time I found the egg adhering to the pan, and stirred more vigorously, thinking by so doing to accomplish the desired object. But when I attempted to turn the omelet, it stuck fast, and wouldn't fold; so I worried over and scraped at it, until all form and comeliness were lost, and it was nothing but a shabby specimen of scrambled eggs. Then I generously left it all for Bridget's breakfast.

"'In despair I went to my friend, who was surprised at my failure; but, to my great delight, she said, "Stay to lunch, and I will make an omelet so that you may see just how it is done." I watched carefully every movement, and kept saying, "*I* did precisely so," until stirring time came. Then my interest grew intense. Placing the omelet in the pan, she set it over moderate heat, and waiting just about a minute, dipped in the fork. Finding the egg had set, or slightly cooked upon the bottom of the pan, she lifted or picked it up, here and there, at various points,— each time raising her fork entirely out of the omelet, and dipping it in at another point. Light dawned. I saw the secret of the whole thing was in this peculiar moving of the omelet as it cooked; and in my amazement, I exclaimed, "And *that* performance you call stirring? I might have tried till doomsday, from your directions, and wouldn't have cooked the omelet properly." "Well, if it isn't stirring — what is it? What would *you* call it?" "Lifting would express the idea more correctly," I replied. "It is lifting the cooked egg that adheres to the pan, so that the uncooked egg may take its place. The egg forms a thin layer or cake on the pan, and dipping the fork in here and there at various points and lifting, loosens the whole mass. The effects produced by stirring and lifting are very different, and in the manfacture of an omelet are very apparent." When a second layer had cooked, the lifting operation was repeated, and so on until the cooked egg filled the pan, and there was no more to be let underneath. In this delicate process of lifting lies the whole secret of the operation. Done in this manner, the butter is not stirred away from the bottom of the pan, and enough remains to allow the omelet to brown nicely, and prevent it from sticking. Since that memorable day I have never failed in making an omelet that gave me entire satisfaction.'"

"I had no idea," interrupted Emeline, "such mysteries were hidden away in an omelet. Few of us, I fear, would labor as Mrs. Rose did to discover them."

"No," I replied, "the most of us are too lazy or too careless to do so. We accept the indifferent food that is placed before us, and grumble at the cook for selecting such unpalatable dishes; but never dream the wretched preparations can be improved upon. Mrs. Rose is an exceptional woman, who never rests satisfied with a dish that she thinks she can in any way improve. Her omelets, I know, from having seen and tasted many of them, are unsurpassable. And I am not willing to believe any woman such a natural stupid as to be capable, after reading the minute description given in these graphic experiences, of making a failure of an omelet. Her letter continues:

"'What do you think of this for salad dressing? I have copied it from a recently published cookbook by a very popular writer. Here is the dressing for "two full grown chickens and three bunches of celery": "Two cups boiling water, two tablespoonfuls of corn-starch wet with cold water, two tablespoonfuls of oil, one cup of vinegar, two teaspoonfuls of made mustard, one great spoonful of fat, skimmed from the liquor in which the fowls were boiled, three raw eggs, three hard-boiled eggs, one teaspoonful powdered sugar, one teaspoonful salt, one teaspoonful pepper, and one teaspoonful Worcestershire sauce." I prefer my salad with a less elaborate dressing. But there is no accounting for tastes, and there are persons, perhaps, who would relish such a concoction. This is the best recipe I know for oil dressing for chicken or other salad: For three chickens take the yolks of eight fresh eggs. Put them in an earthen bowl, and with a silver spoon stir gently and slowly, round and round. Don't beat them. Drop in oil, drop by drop at first, then in small quantities, and very slowly, until in the course of an hour you have used the whole bottle of oil.

At last add three tablespoonfuls of vinegar, two of made mustard, a teaspoonful of salt, and cayenne pepper to taste, continuing the stirring slowly all the while. Prepare the chickens by boiling whole. Salt the water in which they boil, very slightly. Cut the chickens when cold into small bits, half an inch in length, and reject the skin and fibrous pieces. Cut the celery in pieces the same size, and have two-thirds as much celery as chicken. Put the chicken and celery, when thus prepared, in an earthen bowl, and mix well with a fork. Add the dressing just before serving.'"

"I have no doubt Mrs. Rose's recipe for salad dressing is very nice, and for those who like oil, unexceptionable. In my cook-book, in connection with hers, I will give the following recipe: Take the yolks of eight fresh eggs, and one gill each of strong cider-vinegar and water. Heat, to boiling, the vinegar and water, and pour slowly over the beaten yolks, continuing to beat while adding the hot liquid. Put the mixture in an earthen bowl, and set on the range or stove, in a pan of boiling water. Let the water boil around the bowl until the contents are cooked. Stir frequently, and after it begins to thicken, continuously, until done, when remove at once, and continue the stirring for a minute, while cooling. Do not cook it enough to curdle it. Add mustard, pepper, and salt, to taste. When cold, thin to the consistency desired with sweet cream. If cream cannot be had, add an ounce of butter while the dressing is hot; and use sweet milk to thin it when cold. This dressing may be kept in a cool place several days. But when so kept, the cream or milk must not be added till wanted for use. It is excellent for cold slaw, lettuce, etc.

"Kate, don't forget to give a recipe for frizzling beef, in your book," said Emeline, as I laid down Mrs. Rose's letter. "Frizzled beef is a dish much used in warm weather, especially by country people, and, although so simple, it is often unfit to eat by reason of being badly prepared. Instead of being shaved, the beef is cut in thick slices or chunks, and the outer rind left on, which gives it, when cooked, a strong, rank taste. It is then boiled in a quantity of water until all the juice is extracted, and the meat rendered tough and insipid, and flour and strong butter is added to make gravy; or the water is allowed to boil away, and is replaced with skimmed milk. As fond as I am of frizzled beef, I confess I have no relish for it when prepared in the ordinary slip-shod method.

"I am glad you mentioned this delicious breakfast dish. You shall have some in a few days, cooked according to my recipe. Here it is: Cut away all the rind, or dried skin, from as much of the meat as you wish to use. It can then be shaved or sliced easily, and as thin as desired, if a sharp, thin-bladed knife be used. Put a piece of butter in the pan in which it is to be cooked; and when the butter is boiling hot, throw in the shaved beef. Place over a quick fire, and with a fork stir it constantly, to prevent burning. As soon as it looks frizzled or cooked, remove to a cooler place. Dash in a spoonful of flour. Mix well by stirring. Then add a little sweet milk. The amount of butter and milk used must be regulated by the quantity of meat, as in frizzled beef one wants no gravy independent of beef—the beef and gravy should be so assimilated as to render a separation almost impossible. Beef will cook or frizzle by this method in two minutes. Dried mutton, veal, etc., are very nice when cooked this way. Many persons think a little dried liver, shaved in the same manner as the beef, and cooked with it, improves the dish. Be careful to have all mould and outside skin pared or scraped off before putting the meat in the pan, as a very little mould will impart a disagreeable flavor to a large dish of frizzled beef."

"But, Cousin Kate," interrupted Alice, "ma appears to take so much interest in culinary matters this morning, that I'm afraid, unless some one makes a move, the greater part of the day will pass before we finish breakfast." And she left us and tripped lightly up stairs to her room.

After her departure, I said to Emeline, "I have a letter here from my old friend Jennie — I mean Mrs. Douglas — in which she writes: 'Be not startled if we should surprise you some fine morning, by dropping in upon you at Maplewood. How charming it will be to find you in the old home to welcome us. Don't think of going sooner than you intended because of our anticipated return. Gerald joins me in insisting that you and your friends shall remain, as you proposed, till autumn. You mention these friends simply as "Mrs. Richmond and daughter." Have I ever met them? The name has a familiar sound; and yet I can't recall them.'"

"How annoying!" said Emeline. "To be turned out of such comfortable quarters before we get fairly started at our literary labors, is really too bad. But, of course, we must go. I couldn't think of remaining, under all the circumstances."

Questioning in my mind what mystic meaning might be hidden in the latter part of her sentence, I replied: "Don't decide upon anything hastily; and say nothing to Alice, at present, about the matter. Because, as Jennie writes, Gerald's moods may change, — he is so restless and unhappy, — and with them, all their plans. If they decide positively to come home, she promises to give ample notice before they sail. I dare say, however, they'll remain abroad another year."

CHAPTER IX.

IN THE ORCHARD.

We were in the orchard looking for apples to eat, to bake, and to make into pies; and with baskets well filled with Sweets, and Codlings, and Queens, Emeline and I sat under the shade of a tree, while Alice wandered farther on in search of fruit that was rosier-cheeked, or more golden, than any we had gathered.

"Did it ever occur to you, Kate," said Emeline, breaking the silence into which we had fallen, "that there is a universal disposition among all classes of people to wait on the future, and make little account of the present? Most of us fail to enjoy the present, we are so occupied in preparing for the future. In consequence of this feeling we store our closets with preserved fruits, which are in a measure dead fruits, the life, the pure air and sunshine having been crushed and cooked out of them in the process of canning and preserving. When winter comes our cellars are filled with fragrant, delicious apples; so full of goodness that they make the atmosphere, even of a close, damp cellar, redolent of sweetness. But, in our blind stupidity, we pass by, with a careless word of commendation, the very prince of fruits, the apple, leaving it to wither and decay, while we feed on the husks of the past, the cherries and berries and peaches and plums that we have canned and preserved and pickled. How foolish it does seem to neglect the apple, when it is in its very prime, through the fall and winter months, for these fussed-up favorites, which are far less nutritious; and which we ate far too sparingly in their natural state, and while in season, during the sultry summer-time."

"Yes, Emeline, it often seems to me that in caring for the future we waste much of the present. Do you know, by the way, some wise people hold that apples contain all forms or kinds of nutriment essential to sustain and nourish our bodies, and that we can live and thrive upon apples alone, if we use them cooked and uncooked, as food? For the past week I have been thinking about the best methods of canning, preserving, and cooking fruits, and the very thoughts you express have occurred to me. If people were wise enough to eat plentifully of the different kinds of fruits in their proper season, there would be comparatively little need of canning and preserving, in many sections of our country."

"You may be correct in your views, Kate; but since people will can and preserve fruits for some generations yet, I hope you will tell them how to do it according to the best methods. Many persons care little for cooked apples, I think, for the simple reason that they are generally cooked so wretchedly. Sometimes we get them half-baked, and at others we have them in a wishy-washy, watery sauce, so overdosed with sugar and nutmeg, or other heavy spices, that they nauseate delicate stomachs."

"Thank you, Emeline. You give me a hint for my book: *Never spice fruits lest you destroy their flavor.* I always detested nutmeg, allspice, and cinnamon, in apple-pies. I now see the reason. Rich spices and delicate-flavored fruits form an unsuitable and inartistic combination. Heavy spices belong legitimately to heavy sweetness, such as cake, custard, and pumpkin-pie. But the fine, delicate flavor of fruits should be preserved as perfectly as possible; and for this reason they should never be cooked in tin, or stirred with a metal spoon less pure than silver. A wooden spoon or spatula is the best for the purpose.

"These are the directions I shall give: If it is desirable to add to the flavor of the fruit you are cooking, add the flavor of another fruit. For instance, flavor apples with either pineapple, strawberry, raspberry, quince, lemon, or orange, etc. Even the perfume of flowers, like rosewater, may add to the deliciousness of a dish of fruit. But to bury roses in cake, seems as inappropriate and unnatural as to deaden fruit with spices. In cooking fruits of all sorts, whether for present or future use, aim to preserve the flavor of the fruit as far as possible; and to this end, avoid all contact with tin or base metal, and all needless exposure to the air. Cook as soon as possible after the fruit is in proper condition. Cook in small quantities. Simmer gently, instead of boiling rapidly. The flavor of some fruits is preserved better by canning them without sugar. Peaches and blackberries are finer flavored when canned without sugar. At the time of opening and serving, sugar can be added, if desired. Currants and raspberries, when made into jams and jellies, should be simmered until nearly cooked before the sugar is added.

"There is a general impression that sugar is required for canning fruit. This is a mistake. The conveniences for canning are so perfect nowadays that it is not necessary to add sugar to fruit for the purpose of preserving, but only to render it palatable. All fruits will keep perfectly well without sugar, when properly canned. They should be put up boiling hot, in air-tight glass cans; and, unless placed in a dark closet, should be wrapped in thick brown or dark paper, to exclude the light, which changes the color of some fruits, and injures the flavor of others.

Strawberries, and perhaps some other very acid fruits, are best when sugar is added at the time of cooking. Emeline, have you ever seen in any cook-book a recipe for making mushes or jellies of fruit by the addition of arrowroot, corn-starch, or wheat flour?"

"No, I never heard of such a thing until you served us those delicious strawberry, raspberry, and blackberry mushes, as you called them. And you have never yet given us the method of preparing them. Will you repeat it for my benefit?"

"To a quart of berries, fresh or canned, add a pint of water, and sugar to taste. Boil slightly, just enough to cook the fruit; and when nearly done, add corn-starch, arrowroot, or wheat flour, wet with cold water, to thicken the juice and form a mush or jelly of the fruit. Serve cold, with sweet cream."

"Kate, I never ate a more delicate, delicious dessert than these fruit mushes, and they alone ought to render your book popular. What a charming dish for children and invalids, either strawberry, raspberry, or blackberry mush must make! I am surprised I never heard of fruit-mush before this summer."

"Emeline, I think currant jam very much nicer than currant jelly. It has a fresher, better flavor, which I presume is on account of its not being beaten and bruised, and then squeezed through a rag. For jam, bruise the fruit in an earthen bowl, just enough to break the skins and set the juice free. Put in a preserving-kettle. Simmer gently for twenty minutes, skimming carefully, after it begins to boil. At the expiration of the twenty minutes add three-fourths of a pound of white sugar to each pint of crushed currants. Simmer two or three minutes longer, and put in glass cans or jars. One part red raspberries to four parts currants, changes, and, for many persons, improves the flavor."

"A great many ladies," observed Emeline, "have trouble in making jelly; and I hope you will be able to make clear the reason why it sometimes is jelly and sometimes is not, when precisely the same method is followed."

"The same method might be followed in making," I replied, "and yet very different conditions exist. For instance, the fruit might have been gathered at the wrong time, or the sugar have been imperfect. Currants should be gathered for jelly before they are fully ripe; as soon as red, and soft enough for the juice to run freely. Bruise the currants and squeeze through a strong cloth. Measure the juice, and put not more than five pints in the preserving-kettle at once. Simmer gently for twenty minutes after it begins to simmer, skimming it meanwhile. Then add one pound of best loaf sugar for each pint of juice.

Stir, and as soon as perfectly dissolved, and the jelly has boiled up once, remove and put into glasses. Cover when cold. It is well to warm the sugar while the juice is simmering, as that hastens the process. When the fruit is gathered at the right time, and the sugar perfect in quality, this method will always insure perfect jelly, of a beautiful color."

"Kate, as your skill is to be tested to-day in making my favorite among pies, I shall, when we go into the house, read you what Beecher, in 'Eyes and Ears,' says on the subject of apple-pie."

When our pie was placed on the table at dinner, Emeline got her book and read,—

"There is, for example, one made without under-crust, in a deep plate, and the apples laid in in full quarters; or the apples, being stewed, are beaten to a mush and seasoned and put between the double paste; or they are sliced thin and cooked entirely within the covers; or they are put, without seasoning, into their bed, and when baked, the upper lid is raised and the butter, nutmeg, cinnamon, and sugar are added, the whole well mixed, and the crust returned as if nothing happened. But oh, be careful of the paste! Let it be not like putty, nor rush to the other extreme, and make it so flaky that one holds his breath while eating, for fear of blowing it away. Let it not be plain as bread, nor yet rich like cake. Aim at that glorious medium in which it is tender, without being too fugaciously flaky; short, without being too short; a mild, sapid, brittle thing, that lies upon the tongue, so as to let the apple strike through and touch the papillæ with a more affluent flavor. But this, like all high art, must be a thing of inspiration or instinct. A true cook will understand us, and we care not if others do not!

"Do not suppose that we limit the apple-pie to the kinds and methods enumerated. Its capacity in variation is endless, and every diversity discovers some new charm or flavor. It will accept almost every flavor of every spice. And yet nothing is so fatal to the rare and higher graces of apple-pie as inconsiderate, vulgar spicing. It is not meant to be a mere vehicle for the exhibition of these spices, in their own natures; it is a glorious unity, in which sugar gives up its nature as sugar, and butter ceases to be butter, and each flavorsome spice gladly vanishes from its own full nature, that all of them, by a common death, may rise into the new life of apple-pie! Not that apple is longer apple! *It*, too, is transformed; and the final pie, though born of apple, sugar, butter, nutmeg, cinnamon, lemon, is like none of these, but the compound ideal of them all, refined, purified, and by fire fixed in blissful perfection."

"Now," remarked Emeline, "let us see if this is equal to H. W. B.'s ideal pie!"

As she pressed the upper-crust gently with the pie-knife, the merest drop of candied juice appeared between its parted lips; and, although she lifted a piece to another plate with a quick, dexterous movement, a spoon was needed to dip from the pie-dish some juice, unavoidably spilled in the operation. Helping each of us in a similar manner, Emeline ate a minute in silence, and then said, with a satisfied air,—

"Had brother Beecher eaten one of your pies, Kate, before he wrote that essay on apple-pie, he would not for the world have mentioned nutmeg, allspice, or cinnamon, in connection with apple-pie. He would have known they were of the earth earthy, mere 'inconsiderate, vulgar spicing;' good enough, perhaps, for uncultivated or depraved tastes; but not like this, hinting of orange-groves and fairer climes,— a combination of flavors and fragrance unknown to common mortals, who have never enjoyed such a perfect pie as the one now before us. Do tell us how this was fashioned, created, built up into such completeness?"

"Then, I suppose you wish to know, in the first place, how the crust is made?"

"Certainly. That is the body or flesh of a pie. The fruit is the heart, soul, and spirit. I wish to know how the crust and the fruit are compounded; how dough and apple are metamorphosed into a perfect apple-pie."

"To make pie-crust, one pound of flour, a quarter pound of lard, a quarter pound of butter, a glass of cold water, a cool pantry or room, and quick movements, are essential. Place half the flour in a little heap on the moulding-board. Cut the lard into, and through it, until quite fine. Add cold water, and stir with the knife. When wet and quite soft, scrape from the board to one side. Sift from the other half of the flour upon the board, till well covered. Lay the dough on it. Roll it out, but be careful not to get it too thin. Spread half the butter over it, and then cover the butter with flour. Fold, and roll out. Put on the remaining butter, and cover with flour. Fold, and roll quite thin. Sift flour lightly on it. Fold, or roll up, and lay it aside. Take a little more than a fourth of the whole for one crust. Flour the board and dough, and roll to the size required. Place upon the tin or dish, shaping to the same, and cut off around the edge with a sharp knife. Fill the pie with quarters; or, if the apples are large, with eighths, of tart apples. Roll an upper-crust, and lay it over the apples. Trim it around the edges as before, but do not pinch the two crusts together. If you wish to ornament the crust, let the cuts or marks be upon the upper surface only. Do not cut through so as to make holes at which the steam can escape. Place the pie in a hot oven, so that the paste will bake quickly. When thoroughly baked, if the apples are not perfectly cooked, which can be easily ascertained by lifting the upper-crust at one side and peeping in, lessen the heat, or transfer to a cooler oven, until done. If necessary, you can protect the crust, with paper, from becoming too brown."

"Don't you put water in to cook the apples?" interrupted Alice.

"No. The apples are sufficiently juicy to cook themselves, if the steam and juice are kept confined in the pie, as they will be, if no holes are cut or pricked in the upper-crust. While the pie is baking, put in a cup or small stew-pan the sugar required for it, two or three ounces if the apples are tart, as they should be, a small piece of butter, and the juice of an orange, with a very little of the outside grated, if you like it. Melt all together; and, when the pie comes from the oven, slip it from the tin or dish on which it was baked, to the warmed plate on which it is to be served. Lift off the upper-crust. Pour your seasoning over the apple, distributing it evenly; replace the upper-crust, press it gently, and, in one hour the pie is at its best. A pie baked in this manner does not, however, lose its goodness within an hour. The next day, and the day after even, you will find it something more than 'a corpse of an apple-pie.' For four pies, if the apples are not very tart, and you like a rich pie, use the juice of one lemon with that of two oranges and a little grated peel, adding sugar in proportion. Most delicious apple-pies are made by using one grated pineapple to four pies. Place the grated pineapple with the butter and sugar in the stew-pan, and heat to boiling, then add as before, laying it lightly and evenly over the apple, which is permeated by the mixture, without being stirred."

"Mamma," said Alice, "you have heard of cambric tea. Did you ever hear of linen pie?"

"Oh, yes. I have heard people call hot water, with cream and sugar to taste, by that name. They say Horace Greeley used to consider cambric tea a delightful beverage. I drink it sometimes myself; but I believe I have never tasted linen pie. How is it made?"

"Cousin Kate makes it in this way. Instead of filling her pie-crust with apple, or other fruit, she fills it with pieces of old white linen, and bakes. Meanwhile, on the range she prepares the fruit, if it is desirable to cook it; and, when the crust is baked, she slips it on a plate, lifts off the upper-crust, takes out the rags, and fills their place with the juicy fruit, which couldn't possibly be baked in the pie, without losing a large portion of the juice, and spoiling the looks, as well as the taste of the pie. At dinner every one who doesn't understand the trick wonders how so juicy a pie was so perfectly baked. And no one can imagine how the upper-crust was baked so rich and brown, without being stained with juice, and the under-crust so crisp, without being soaked or heavy. To the uninitiated it is no doubt as great a marvel as the apple inside the dumpling was to the bewildered king, who asked, amazed, 'How got the apple in?'"

"There is another advantage, Alice," I said, "in baking these linen pies. Several crusts may be baked and put away for a day or two unfilled; and an hour or two before serving, if placed for a few minutes in a hot oven, until warmed through, and then filled with fresh fruit, they can scarcely be distinguished from freshly baked pies. These linen pies are just the things to fill with strawberries or other fruit which is good uncooked.

"To change the subject a little, Emeline, I agree fully with the remark you made this morning, that few persons care for cooked apples, because they are, as a general thing, so poorly cooked. The apple, although it contains so many elements of goodness, is one of our most abused fruits. As a general rule, it is shabbily treated in every process of cooking it is compelled to undergo. It is badly baked, and wretchedly stewed. It is diluted with water, or dosed with sugar, or doctored with spices, until all the original flavor is lost, or spoiled. But, in spite of all this bad usage, the apple has retained a place in the culinary department, and is destined, as soon as we learn how to cook it properly, to grow into universal favor, and become a prominent article of diet at every well-ordered table."

"Many persons," observed Emeline, "are of opinion that only sweet apples are good for baking. I, however, like a tart apple, when baked, much better than I do a sweet one. Which do you prefer, Kate? And what is your method of baking apples?"

"I very much prefer sour apples. And this, I think, is the best way of baking them: Take large, juicy sour apples. Pare them, and remove the cores, leaving the apples whole; place them in a deep earthen dish; add to them one tablespoonful of water; put them in a hot oven, and bake until perfectly soft and tender. A few minutes before removing from the oven, sprinkle them lightly with white sugar. They will then brown richly, and have a delicious flavor. Serve warm, hot, or cold, according to taste. Most people soon grow so fond of them as to eat them with their meats and vegetables; and also to take them, garnished with sugar and cream, for dessert, in preference to either pudding or pie.

"To bake apples whole, remove all imperfect spots or specks; pierce the skins in sundry places with a fork; place in an earthen pan or dish, and bake in a hot oven. An apple baked quickly, with all the heat it can bear, is very different from one baked in a moderate oven. The former is spicy and full of spirit, while the latter tastes as if all life had been worried out of it by slow torture.

"Apple sauce, as usually made, is scarcely fit to eat; yet, when properly prepared, it is one of the most delicious dishes of which I have any knowledge. Apples should always be stewed in a porcelain-lined kettle,— never in a vessel made of tin. Very little water should be added to them; and they should not be stirred, if possible to avoid it, while cooking. They should be covered closely, and cooked quickly; and should be watched all the time while cooking, lest they burn. When done, the sugar required should be put into an earthen bowl, and the apple poured over it, and covered closely until served. Stewed apple that is continually stirred while cooking, is not spicy and high-flavored, like that quickly and quietly cooked. If desired to flavor apple sauce with lemon, slice the lemon and put in the dish with sugar, and pour the hot sauce upon it.

Stewed prunes, flavored in the same way with lemon, I think are much improved. Cooking lemon damages the flavor. As a usual thing, too much sugar is used; so much, in fact, that all apple flavor is lost in the heavy sweetness. To preserve the perfect flavor of stewed apples, or apple sauce, great care is required in the judicious use of sugar or spices."

"By the way," said Emeline, "I have somewhere eaten a pudding made of apples and tapioca, that I thought very nice. Have you ever made it?"

"Oh, yes," I replied. "Such a pudding, when properly made, and served cold, is a very delicate dessert. I think to serve it warm, however, as it is often served, is as poor taste as to serve a custard pudding warm. To make tapioca pudding, use five measures of cold water to one measure of tapioca. Let it soak over night, or for several hours; then cook it until it looks clear and transparent. While the tapioca is cooking, pare and core some large greenings, or other tart apples. Leave the apples whole. Place them close together in a deep earthen dish, and pour the tapioca over them. Bake thoroughly, until the apples brown over the top. When quite cold, serve with sugar and sweet cream.

"Another tapioca pudding which is very nice, is made by soaking half a pint of tapioca over night in two quarts cold water. In the morning drain, and boil until cooked in two quarts sweet milk. Salt slightly. Remove from the fire, and add slowly the well-beaten yolks of eight eggs. Stir rapidly while adding the egg. Lastly, sweeten to taste. When cool, flavor with vanilla, lemon, or wine. Beat the whites of the eggs stiff, add pulverized sugar, and serve with the pudding."

"Kate, I notice people eat much more fruit than they used to, with their meals. A few years ago one never saw melons, peaches, grapes, berries, or any kind of fruit at meal-time, except as dessert for dinner. Now, a great many families make the principal part of their breakfast of such articles, and also eat liberally of them at their other meals."

"Yes, I am glad to see the improvement in this respect. Nearly all, perhaps all classes of people crave green food; and it seems to me the craving ought to be gratified, by their making fruits and vegetables a part of their regular daily diet. When people eat freely of fruits, at their regular meals, as they do other articles of diet, they have little disposition to indulge in the injurious habit of eating between meals; while, on the other hand, in families where such things are seldom served at meal-time, men, women, and children hanker after unripe fruit even; and render themselves liable to all manner of diseases by eating green apples, half-ripe cherries and berries, and trash generally.

"In one of her letters to me, Mrs. Rose writes: 'I never put sugar *on* berries for tea. It spoils the shape of the berries to let them lie in or under sugar.' Now, there is no doubt it spoils the shape of berries to sugar them; but, for most persons, it improves the flavor to sprinkle them with sugar ten or fifteen minutes before the berries are served. No one disputes the orthodoxy of Mr. Beecher's opinions on gustatory matters, however much they may differ from him on theological subjects, and *he* approves of mashing them even. He says: 'Put ripe berries in a dish, add a little *cold water*, break them down with a spoon to a jelly, adding just enough sugar and water to make them half liquid, and you shall find many another dish less delicious.' This disposition to preserve the shape of articles of food is quite prevalent among housewives; and the taste of many a dish is sacrificed, in order that it may make a handsome appearance on the table. Fruits, grains, and vegetables are too often purposely sent to table half cooked, so that the shape may not be spoiled. In all such cases the eye is gratified at the expense of the stomach. The idea that these articles, when ready for the table, should present the same form and appearance as when uncooked, is, in my judgment, a very erroneous one. Food of every kind should be thoroughly cooked — even though in the operation all form and comeliness be destroyed — as it is then more palatable and nutritious to healthy stomachs. There is, however, a vast difference between thorough cooking and too much cooking. Food is as effectually spoiled by too much as by too little cooking; and any one wishing to excel in culinary science must note carefully the distinction, and strike the happy medium. If vegetables were properly cooked, and fruits properly prepared for the table, they could scarcely fail to be always acceptable to the average appetite, and would soon force themselves into general use. I may be too enthusiastic; but I look forward hopefully to the time when they will be so cooked and prepared; and when cartloads of vegetables will be consumed where an occasional mess is now deemed sufficient; and when fruits, cooked and uncooked, will be considered as essential to a meal as bread or meat."

After dinner Emeline and I were on the veranda, chatting in an indolent, indifferent way, on various topics, when Alice appeared with the small gilt-edged volume, and interrupted us by saying,—

"Mamma, I've brought this 'Memoir of Helen Douglas,' to read you some extracts. I have always detested memoirs, and thought them the stupidest of books, calculated only to bore amiable and well-disposed people. But this differs in that respect from the usual memoir. I have marked some passages that I think suggestive as well as beautiful. Shall I read them to you?"

"By all means, if Cousin Kate doesn't object," was Emeline's reply.

"Cousin Kate," I said, "will be delighted to hear them."

Alice then read: —

"'To the average mind the idea of immortal life presents itself simply as a continuation, after death, of the life we have lived in this world, extending through eternity; free, however, from all the cares and sorrows, all the pains and infirmities, of this mortal existence. But if we retain our personal consciousness in eternity, will we not retain also the faculties that were essential to our development in time? Or will all our emotions, passions, feelings, be sloughed off with our flesh by death? How will we recognize beyond the grave those whom we loved so fondly here? Will my lost Helen meet me years hence the same gentle being that went from my sorrowing gaze? Or will she be changed, re-created, formed anew? How shall I know her

"—— in the land that keeps
The disembodied spirits of the dead"?

Or what assurance have I that our love shall not

change with a change of existence? O God, why am I tormented with these painful questionings?'

"'Whence do we come, or whither do we go? No one can answer satisfactorily. It is an unsolvable riddle. All guesswork, speculation. Joy and happiness are mere illusions—the flickering sunshine of a moment. Pain is a reality. The only tangible thing in life is suffering, sorrow.'

"'Since Helen died, all things seem changed. When she was alive I looked eagerly forward. The future seemed bright and beckoning. So full of great hopes, of grand possibilities. My hours were crowded with work. The days were too short to satisfy me, I had so much to do. Now I dare not look backward, I care not to look forward. To do either seems like peering into the gloom of a winter's night. The present is full of heaviness. I cannot set myself to any task, and thus escape from my great grief, for nothing now seems worth the doing.'

"'Will the days ever come when I can realize—

"'Tis better to have loved and lost,
Than never to have loved at all"?

Life is poor and barren without love; but how painfully desolate it becomes after the loss of the one loved better than all else on earth! I was the victim of unrest before love entered, and took possession of my heart; nevertheless, I was negatively happy. Now, my days and nights are filled to overflowing with sorrow. A weary life is mine to bear.'

"' Now that Helen has been torn from me, after so short a season of unalloyed happiness, I tremble at the thought of annihilation, and refuse to believe the gloomy doctrine. Yet, I can find no satisfying evidence of the soul's immortality,— nothing to convince my mind, beyond a doubt, that there is a world and a life beyond the tomb. Love, however, uproots disbelief. Selfishness is more satisfying than reason. The yearning to be again with Helen dispels doubt, and overturns argument. We must, we will, meet again. But is this life to be projected into the next, with all its hates, as well as all its loves? If with the one, why not with the other? And why should a continuation of such a mutual love as ours be vouchsafed to us, if thousands are doomed to go wailing through eternity, sorrowing for an unrequited or a hopelessly lost affection? Oh, Helen, Helen, why did we ever love?'

"' The death of Helen was so sudden, so unexpected, that I was nearly bereft of reason by the terrible blow. I was sometimes saddened by the thought of dying and leaving her alone in the world; but I had never thought of death in connection with Helen. It is ever thus in life. The evils we apprehend, and most dread, are seldom the ones that befall us. Fate seems to delight in taking us by surprise,—in tripping us suddenly into an unseen abyss.'

"'Oh, my lost, loved one! Is there anything in life that can compensate for the agonies I have suffered since your frail, inanimate form was carried to the snow-covered graveyard? The world may be full of beauty, but I neither see nor enjoy it without you. Why was I permitted to love you with such an all-absorbing love, that when you went out of life you took with you all its sunshine and fragrance? Can it be that "He doeth all things well?" Though my lips give utterance to the expression, my heart refuses to acknowledge His goodness. Wherein lies the goodness of the blow that has so cruelly deprived me of my earthly treasure? Does such merciless sorrow as mine benefit me, or the world? Is it essential to the happiness of a future life, that this one should be so full of suffering?'

"'To-day I gazed down from the mountain-tops upon a scene of surpassing loveliness. And I asked, How many men and women within the whole scope of my vision are capable of enjoying this glorious prospect? Not the weary laborers, who are toiling and sweating in the fields to earn a bare subsistence; not the wealthy possessors of all these farms and houses, who are insanely struggling to amass more and more wealth; not the aimless wanderers, with blighted or broken lives, vainly endeavoring to flee away from their own wretchedness. A favored few there may be, perhaps, who enjoy it in a measure. But even they have no lease of happiness, and no security for their enjoyment continuing beyond the passing moment. Those who are happiest to-day may to-morrow be overwhelmed with grief as crushing and poignant as mine. Why, then, do we exist? Or why were we created? Why are the vast majority of the earth's inhabitants born only to struggle and toil, to suffer and weep? Can it be that we are born for a brief life, filled mostly with unhappiness, or, at the best, with only negative happiness, and that we then drop out of existence forever?'

"'This morning the preacher took for a text, "It is a fearful thing to fall into the hands of the living God." And his sermon seemed to me like blasphemy. Are we not always in God's hands? Does he ever let any one drop out of his protecting arms? Can it be that we slip from his grasp when death overtakes us? Banish the thought. I will not entertain it. The preacher did not realize what he said. It would be a fearful thing to fall *out* of the hands of the living God. Only in his loving embrace do we rest secure.'"

"'The Meditations of Gerald Douglas,' it seems to me," interrupted Emeline, "would be a more appropriate title for the volume than 'A Memoir of Helen Douglas.'"

"O no, ma," said Alice, "I have only read you some of the reflections suggested to his mind while preparing the memoir of his dead wife. Let me read you a portion of the memoir itself."

"Not now, Alice," was the quiet reply of her mother; "it is no doubt beautifully written, but I think you have read enough for the present. Let us take a ramble."

CHAPTER X.

EDIBLES AND EDUCATION.

"Egg-plant?" interrogatively remarked Cousin Emeline, as we took our seats at the table. "This must be a new and early variety?"

"Yes," I replied, as I passed her a slice of the fried vegetable. "I wish your opinion as to whether it is equal in quality to that which comes later in the season."

There was a merry twinkle in Alice's eye, which her mother did not notice, as she answered, —

"Why, this is delicious! I never ate finer egg-plant. Indeed, I think this has a delicacy of flavor I never before observed in the vegetable. Have you some new process of cooking it, by which you extract that peculiar flavor which renders egg-plant obnoxious to many persons?"

"No," I said, giving Alice a silencing glance. "This was fried in the same manner in which I usually fry egg-plant. Cut in slices a quarter of an inch in thickness, rubbed lightly with salt, and piled one slice upon another that some of the water might be drawn from the plant, it was allowed to stand for half an hour. The slices were then wiped dry, dusted very lightly with pepper, and freely with flour, and fried until thoroughly done, and nicely brown, in a small quantity of fat. For frying nearly everything of this sort, a thick cast-iron pan or spider is much better than one made of lighter metal. Equal proportions of lard and butter I find better for frying than either lard or butter alone. A small quantity should be first placed in the pan or spider, and, when hot, the slices of vegetables should be laid in. When nicely browned they should be turned, and more of the butter and lard added. Egg-plant will soak a great deal of fat, if permitted to do so. I therefore put in at first only enough to fry one side; and add sparingly, from time to time, as is necessary. It is well to have a cup of this butter and lard mixture at hand, melted and hot, so that you can put it in the pan when required. To prevent the slices soaking fat, some cooks coat them with egg and bread-crumbs; but I can't see that anything is gained by the operation, as the coating absorbs a good deal of grease, which is eaten with the egg-plant; and when cooked in this way it is liable to be underdone, as it requires much more cooking with, than without the coating of crumbs. I also think it far more palatable without the crumbs; but as tastes differ, there is no harm in trying both methods."

"I am exceedingly fond of egg-plant fried without egg and crumbs," observed Emeline, "and think it one of the best of breakfast-dishes. With me it takes the place of meat. May I trouble you for another slice?"

"Give ma fried squash this time, Cousin Kate," said Alice, adding in a mock tone of pity, "Poor mamma! to be victimized in this way, and made to praise fried squash so enthusiastically, all for the sake of Cousin Kate's horrid cook-book, is too bad! It is positively cruel, I declare!"

"Fried squash!" interrupted Emeline. "What do you mean?"

"Why simply this," I explained. "That summer squash, or cymlin, when fried in the same manner as egg-plant, is a good substitute —"

"And not always detected as a substitute," interrupted Alice, mischievously. "In fact, is sometimes mistaken for the genuine article by those very fond of egg-plant."

"Which means, I suppose," said Emeline, "that this delicious dish I have been eating and praising, is fried squash, — something I never heard of before."

"Exactly," I rejoined; "and by many preferred to egg-plant, on account of being a less hearty food, and having a more delicate flavor. Tomatoes, not over-ripe, cut in thick slices, and fried in the same manner, are very nice. The tomato should be sliced, seasoned, dusted with flour, and fried immediately. The skin should be left on, to prevent the slices from coming to pieces."

"Kate," said Emeline, "you certainly excel as a fryer, — or, fryist, or whatever the proper term may be. From fried chicken down to fried squash, all your fries are admirable; and if your methods were generally adopted, such a revolution would take place in that sadly abused mode of preparing food, that the frying-pan would again come into as general use as in the days of our grandmothers. Oysters fried after your recipe I always forget to praise, in my eagerness to enjoy."

"And yet, Emeline, I have in several instances given my exact method of frying oysters to friends, and when the black, greasy things came upon the table, although I could not recognize them as the legitimate result of my method at all, the hostess invariably insisted that my directions had been followed to the minutest particular. This is a somewhat discouraging experience for one contemplating writing a cook-book. Nevertheless, I suppose I shall go on telling people how to cook, and hopefully look to the future for better results.

"For frying oysters, I like cracker-crumbs rolled very fine and sifted, so that you have almost cracker-flour. The oysters should be taken singly, and well rinsed in their own liquor, or in cold water, so that no particle of shell shall adhere to them, and laid upon a sieve or folded napkin, to drain. While the oysters are draining, season the cracker-crumbs with salt and cayenne pepper. Mix the seasoning very thoroughly with the cracker-dust; dip each oyster in well-beaten egg, and roll it freely in the cracker. Lay it on a plate, or board, convenient to handle. Prepare in this way all the oysters before you begin to fry. A thick dripping-pan or deep griddle answers well for frying them in. When everything is ready, place in the pan an ounce or two of lard. The exact quantity required depends upon the size of the pan and the number of oysters. When the lard is boiling hot, add to it an equal quantity of butter. As soon as the butter is melted and mixed with the lard, fill the pan with oysters, laying them close together. Let the heat be enough to fry quickly, but not so great as to burn. When brown on one side, turn the oysters; and when nicely brown on both sides, lift to a heated platter, and serve immediately. Fried oysters, chicken, potatoes, etc., are supposed to be nicer served on a napkin.

"It is well to let the lard get hot in the pan before the butter is added, as the butter is not so likely to scorch as when put in the pan at first. Place enough of the mixture in the pan before you begin frying, to fry the oysters on both sides; but if a second panful is to be fried, the pan must be washed, and all the burnt grease removed, or the oysters will be badly damaged by it. When properly cooked, the oyster comes to the table of a light brown color, thinly coated all over with crumbs,— not warm, greasy, and leathery, but hot and juicy, and tasting precisely like — a fried oyster!

"For scalloped oysters, prepare the crumbs by drying bread very thoroughly in a cool oven. Broken pieces and crusts will answer as well as whole slices, if the bread is of good quality and the crusts not brown. Several hours will be required to dry the bread sufficiently; and it will not be injured if lightly browned in the process. When dried, roll it very fine, rejecting whatever will not crush into fine crumbs. Season the crumbs well with salt, pepper, and butter, rubbing all between the hands until thoroughly mixed. Rinse and drain the oysters the same as for frying. The dish in which scalloped oysters are cooked should be shallow,— holding not more than three or four layers of oysters and crumbs. Scatter a thin layer of crumbs over the bottom of the dish, and place a layer of oysters upon them. Over these scatter a thin layer of crumbs, and lay in more oysters. So fill the dish, covering each layer of oysters with a layer of crumbs. Over the top, place the crumbs thickly, so as to form a coating or crust, which will protect the oysters from exposure. It requires three-quarters of an hour to cook scalloped oysters three or four layers deep. The oven should be hotter than for bread — hot enough to cook as quickly as possible without burning the crumbs. The dish should be of a rich brown all over the top, before it is moved from the oven; and when served, the oysters should be plump and juicy. The juice, however, should be found inside the oysters,— while on the outside they should be so dry as to roll and tumble about on the plate. They should not be wet, sticky, and packed together; nor shrunken, leathery, and sloppy, from too much moisture, and from slow cooking or over-cooking. Oysters — whether stewed, fried, scalloped, or broiled,— should never be cooked long enough to collapse and become tough and juiceless."

"Kate, in the matter of food, my sympathies are with country people," observed Emeline. "They usually cook their food in such a careless, slovenly manner, and have so little variety in it, that but for their active out-door lives they would certainly lose all appetite, and die of starvation. It is hard to imagine how people manage to survive, who, day after day, for years, drink the sloppy tea and coffee, and eat the sour, heavy bread, and badly cooked meat and vegetables one is treated to at the average country house! But the worst of it all is that they worry through life on such fare, and never realize the fact that it is possible to prepare food in any better way. Your cook-book will give them some useful hints on preparing frizzled beef, picked-up codfish, and many other staple dishes of plain, wholesome food. And I trust you will also tell them how to make decent fish-balls. There is such a vast difference between a perfect fish-ball and a fish-ball as ordinarly made and cooked, that I think the subject deserves special mention."

"Yes," I replied, "the difference between an ordinary and a perfect fish-ball, is as marked and appreciable as between any other properly and improperly prepared article of food. To make perfect fish-balls requires care and attention. Salt fish should be soaked for several hours in cold water, then boiled slowly until very tender. The potatoes should be well boiled, dry, and mealy. Take measure for measure of fish picked clean from skin and bones, and potatoes. Add a fresh egg, a small piece of butter, Cayenne pepper, and a little sweet milk. Work these ingredients so perfectly together that the fish and potato are as indivisible as are two drops of water run together. In this thorough mixing consists the chief art of making fish-balls. Roll this mixture into round balls between the hands, dust with flour, and fry in boiling lard. If the balls crack and come to pieces in the lard, it is because the lard is not hot enough or the balls are too soft. These round balls, fried in a quantity of boiling lard, will be found far superior, for most tastes, to flat cakes made of the same fish and fried in a small amount of grease. When nicely brown, the ball should be lifted from the lard in a wire skimmer, dried on a napkin, and served hot. When boiled fish, with drawn butter, has been served for dinner, what is left can be made into balls, and the gravy used instead of butter and milk. Delicious balls can also be made of fresh fish, either baked or boiled, and a proportion of light bread soaked in sweet milk may be used in place of potato."

"Can't you also suggest," asked Emeline, " some improvement in hashes and warmed-up meats and potatoes? They are so often found upon breakfast-tables, in both city and country, that every one should be acquainted with the best manner of preparing them."

"All cold fresh meats, when properly hashed and served, make nice, palatable breakfast-dishes. In preparing them, great care should be taken to throw out all gristle, tough skin, and dry, chippy portions. The meat should then be hashed fine, and mixed either with hashed potato or bread crumbed and soaked in sweet milk. Ordinary hash, made of equal proportions of corned beef and potato, can be much improved and made really delicious, by adding bread-crumbs soaked in milk, or sweet milk or cream without the crumbs, and working it well with the hand, then forming it into rolls, and browning in the oven. Or, it may be placed in a well-buttered bread-pan of medium size, and put in a hot oven until it is brown on the bottom and sides, and perfectly heated. When ready to serve, turn it from the pan on a heated platter. Very nice hashed meat-balls or cakes are made by mixing with hashed meat, bread crumbed and soaked in sweet milk, and a *fresh egg*. Season to taste with salt and pepper, and sweet herbs, if liked. If the meat is mostly lean, sweet cream or a little butter must be added. Make into round cakes, and fry quickly in a small quantity of hot fat. When brown on both sides, serve hot. For frying all these meat-and-potato cakes, the fat fried out of salt pork is much nicer than fresh lard.

"'Scrapple,' made in the following manner, is both palatable and nutritious. Instead of pork, which is generally used for making scrapple, take a piece of beef, or a beef-bone with meat on it, and boil slowly till very tender. Strain the liquor into an earthen bowl, and set aside. Separate the bone from the meat, and when cold, hash the meat fine and put it in a kettle with the liquor and half of the fat that has risen on it. Season with salt and pepper; and when it boils, thicken with corn meal. Stir in the meal as in making mush or hasty pudding. When thick enough, or as thick as mush, pour into a pan to cool; and when cold, cut in slices and fry in a skillet, or on a hot griddle. In cool weather scrapple will keep several days, and is a convenient breakfast-dish.

"Hashed potato warmed, I think much nicer than that which is coarsely sliced. This is my method of preparing it: Place a small piece of butter in the kettle or pan to be used for warming, and when melted, add milk, or thin cream (which is better), with salt and pepper to taste; and lastly, add the hashed potato. Cover closely and set where it will heat slowly. The milk should boil up through and over the potato, and have time to soak into it pretty thoroughly. It should be stirred very little, and when served no milk should be visible. Hashed potato warmed in this manner is very nice with beefsteak, ham, or cold meat.

"Chicken croquettes are very nice for breakfast, lunch, or supper. Do you know how they are made, Kate?" asked Emeline.

"There are more elaborate methods, but this is very nice: Take a chicken, boiled as for salad, or cold roast chicken will answer. Chop fine and place in a stew-pan, with a gill of chicken broth. Season to taste with salt and pepper. Stir to a smooth paste an ounce of butter and tablespoonful of flour, which add to the chicken when boiling. Lastly, add the well-beaten yolks of two eggs, stirring rapidly. Remove at once from the fire. When cold, add minced parsley; mix well. Scatter fine bread-crumbs on the bread-board, and taking a spoonful of chicken roll into any shape desired, rolling in some of the crumbs. When shaped, dip in beaten egg, roll in bread-crumbs, lay in a wire basket, and fry in hot lard the same as chicken, potatoes, etc. The wire basket is also nice for frying potatoes.

"A simple stew that is relished occasionally as a breakfast dish, by most persons, is made in this manner: Put a piece of butter and two or three sliced onions in the stew-pan. Cover, and cook slowly until brown. Add cold meat, roast or boiled, cut in small pieces, and gravy, if you have any; also a quart of ripe tomatoes, fresh or canned, with pepper and salt to taste. Cover closely and simmer gently for two hours; when, if too thin, thicken with a mixture of flour and butter, or flour and sweet cream. Cover the top of the stew with pieces of stale bread, half an inch thick, and two inches square. Simmer a few minutes, and serve on a heated platter, placing the pieces of bread at the bottom, and dishing the stew over it."

"But, as you and I, Kate," said Emeline, rising, "are to go for the mail to-day, isn't it about time to stop our gossip?"

In the afternoon Emeline and I took a long

walk to the village post-office, and, on our way home, sat down to rest under the grand old oak that stands, like a faithful sentinel, at the entrance to Maplewood. Absorbed with my own meditations, I gazed in silence at the beautiful landscape, until my attention was arrested by an impatient exclamation from Emeline, who, in looking over the village paper, which was among our mail-matter, had been irritated by the following paragraph : —

"Personal. — The readers of the 'Democrat' will be glad to learn that our reporter, after thoroughly investigating the affair, has come to the conclusion that there are no 'spooks' in or about the Douglas mansion ; and that the story of ghosts and goblins having been seen and heard there, originated with a nervous old lady, who one evening happened to see some fairy-like garments ornamenting a clothes-line in the garden, and permitted her imagination to get the better of her judgment. The facts in the case, as far as our reporter has been able to gather them, are simply these : Three lady friends of the Douglas family, who are said to belong to the class known as 'strong-minded women,' have been spending the summer at Maplewood, and doing the principal part of their own housework for the sake of privacy and seclusion. Rumor has it that they have been making experiments in cookery, etc., and intend getting up a book, in which instructions will be given for preparing food in a practical manner. We hope this latter report may prove true; for the cook-book has yet to be written in which concise directions are given for plain cooking; and improvements in the cooking of the average American housewife are certainly greatly to be desired. It is said the Douglases intend coming home shortly; and it is also whispered among gossips that one of the present occupants of their mansion is a beautiful young lady, who, travelling with her mother in Switzerland last summer, fell in with the Douglas party; that a sudden attachment sprung up between the young people; and that, ere many months, a new mistress will occupy the old manse."

"Kate," she said, after I had finished reading the obnoxious article, "I'd much rather Alice wouldn't see that. I think it would annoy and vex her exceedingly. And if it did not do that, it might start her on a new train of thought more objectionable than the one she is now pursuing. Do you know the child's behavior astonishes me. Educated in a convent, and always accustomed to the strict formalities of the church, one would naturally suppose she would have been shocked at the doubts and sentiments expressed by Gerald in his ravings about his dead wife. But the other day, when I said something of the sort to her, she simply answered, 'Why so, mamma? I've had very similar thoughts myself. Quite as wicked, I dare say; but I never could have given them such beautiful expression.' I confess to you, Kate, I'm becoming seriously annoyed. I don't like this hero-worship she is evidently indulging in. Why, the child is only twenty; and I should prefer to have her keep clear of love's entangling alliances until she is twenty-five, at least."

"True," I replied, "but you know 'Satan finds some mischief still for idle hands to do.' And that which is true of hands is equally true of brains and hearts. If you don't wish Alice to think about Gerald, and fall in love before her time, give her something else to think about, and something to do. Now, if you were to become heartily enlisted in this school project of mine, who knows but she might join in the work also, and become so enthusiastically interested in it, that love would be put away from her thoughts forever."

"No,—not forever, I hope," said Emeline; "that would be too long. But what is this school project you speak of? Do you seriously contemplate taking charge of a school for girls?"

"Seriously, I do," was my reply. "Heretofore, as you know, I have done a good deal of talking; hereafter, I propose doing some honest work. It seems to me of vital importance that girls should be thoroughly instructed in the domestic arts. Of these, I consider the culinary department the most important. But a practical knowledge of all of them is essential to the comfort and well-being of a household. Glance over the homes to which you have free entrance. Look at the slack, slovenly way in which most of them are ordered. Housework is considered drudgery of the meanest sort, and is pushed aside whenever possible; or, if not, is done in a fretful, complaining spirit. Servants, as a class, are poorly educated in their department; but the average servant who professes to do general housework, is fully up to the capacity of the average mistress. Where a servant habitually makes poor bread, serves badly cooked food, or does her work generally in a sleazy, slipshod manner, you will find the mistress powerless to correct the evils, because of her ignorance of the proper methods. Here, emphatically, 'knowledge is power'; and Bridget misrules the household, because her ignorance is less dense than the ignorance of the mistress. Now, in this school of mine the girls are to be taught home duties and domestic work; and, at the same time, to be inspired with a love of them."

"How?" asked Emeline, all attention.

"Insensibly, in a thousand ways," I continued. "In the first place, the school is to be a home;

and is to be as charming and attractive as it can be made. Everything about it will be convenient, comfortable, cosy. The housekeeping department will be administered with great care; and the girls will see, every day and all the time, housework properly performed. The table will be abundantly supplied with the best food, prepared in the most careful manner, after the most approved methods. In short, my ideas are, that study, under proper conditions, is conducive to thorough health; that the highest mental culture is productive of the most perfect physical development; and that young women, while being qualified for the duties of life, can be developed mentally and physically, and inspired with a genuine, abiding love of domestic as well as intellectual pursuits. Emeline, you may consider me an enthusiast; but I expect to live long enough to see these theories of mine, if you choose to call them such, demonstrated as facts at this Home-School, or home and school combined."

"But, Kate, after you get through with cooking, I don't see what will remain for your girls to learn in the housekeeping department. Every woman of sense knows how to do general housework,—to wash and iron, make beds, sweep, etc."

"No, Emeline; I think very few women know the best ways of doing any of these things. I expect to deliver a lecture, at least once a week, to the girls in the domestic department, on such subjects as — how to make fires, with the special treatment of coal fires; how to manage draughts and dampers; how to keep a coal fire at a low ebb, yet ready to be forced to a quick heat in a few minutes; how to sweep with a common broom without raising a dust; how to make and use baking and ironing holders; how to make beds; and so on, indefinitely. And in this connection let me give you a little story, just in point. One day, when travelling in the West, I fell into conversation with a gentleman who occupied the seat next to mine in the cars. Our talk was rambling and desultory. He, I learned, was President of an Eastern college, who had been spending his vacation in Minnesota. He had a lot of guns and fishing-tackle with him, and had evidently been having a good time. 'What a perfect place,' he said, 'Minnesota is for a summer vacation. The climate is delightful during July and August. How pure and bracing the atmosphere is on the hottest days. And the nights are so delightfully cool, that no one thinks of sleeping without blankets,— double blankets at that.' And here an expression of pain clouded his genial face. After a moment's hesitation, however, he continued: 'I wish something could be done — but I suppose nothing can — to cure chambermaids of a stupid habit they have, which has caused me more serious annoyance during my life, I think, than any other one thing. I've been tempted several times to write a newspaper article upon the subject, and call attention to it as a public and general nuisance, but I have never done so. You may look upon it as a trifle; but I assure you I found it a very serious matter the other night at a hotel in St. Paul. I had been out tramping all day, and came in very tired. The evening was cool; and when I crawled under the blankets at bedtime, I had no presentiment of coming evil. But after a sound sleep, I awoke, sweltering in torments, loaded with blankets. Upon a careful examination I discovered I had been sleeping under two heavy blankets in August. I attempted to turn one away, but found they would not be separated. Both would go, or both would stay. It was dark, and I had no matches; so I tugged, and labored, and toiled; but my efforts to separate the blankets were ineffectual. Eventually I discovered the cause of failure: the stupid chambermaid had put the open ends of the double blankets at the foot, instead of at the head, of the bed. I tried in vain to turn and right them. They were in coils and twists innumerable, and would not be righted. Finally, I slept, from sheer exhaustion; and this horrible cold that annoys me so much, is the result. But that night I swore a solemn oath, never, so long as I live, to go to bed again without having first examined the bed, to see if the blankets are put on right.' The lives of most of us are made up of trifles, that vitality affect our happiness; and the wretched experience of my travelling acquaintance, the Professor, while showing the results of a seemingly trivial matter, forcibly illustrates the importance of knowing how to properly do so small a thing as put blankets on a bed!"

"Indeed, Kate," said Emeline, "I think beds generally, outside of first-class hotels, are an abomination. People spend about one-third of their lives in bed; and what should be a couch of rest, where sleep comes unbidden, is more often a sack of torture,—a humpy, bumpy, sliding, rolling, tormenting thing, so badly made up that you roll and toss, the night through, seeking vainly either rest or sleep. And the sickening odors of 'spare rooms,' or 'guest-chambers,' as they are termed, where weary visitors are put to spend the night on such beds! Bah! they linger in one's memory for years. You will do a good thing in your school, if you impress upon your pupils the necessity of comfortable, well-made beds, and thoroughly aired spare-rooms and parlors."

"Emeline, our pupils will be taught to live in their homes—to occupy their parlors and spare-rooms every day; and to keep them swept and garnished for themselves, and not for occasional guests. Self-respect is one of the first things that should be developed in a boy or girl. And by self-respect I mean the high and honorable feeling that prevents men and women from being mean and narrow to themselves in their daily home life. People who have genuine respect and consideration for themselves, never fail to treat other people with respect and consideration. To learn to be just and respectful to our fellow men and women, we must first learn to be just and respectful to ourselves. I have but little faith in reformers who go about endeavoring to reform society, while they neglect, or are ignorant of, the duties they owe to themselves and their families. Think you, women who consider household work menial and degrading, and whose houses are nurseries of disorder and ill-training, are likely to elevate and advance humanity by their efforts? The true reformer must begin at home, and work outward. And until the average home is reformed and made what it should be, the reformatory movements of our age will mostly end in failure. Here among my letters is one from Mrs. Wheaton, a woman of wealth and culture, who feels that *she* was created for something better than to be 'a household drudge.' She asks, 'Can you suggest any way whereby the wife and mother can make home happy and attractive to husband and sons, without giving her life to the work? — devoting all her powers of mind and body to it? In short, without bringing her mind down to the level of that of a common cook and drudge?' Now, the idea that certain kinds of labor are degrading, while other kinds are refining and elevating, is, I think, a stumbling-block to many. People of education and intelligence seem to lose sight of the fact that it is the heart we put into labor of any kind—the motive that underlies it—that makes its performance either elevating or degrading in its effects. It seems strange to me that people who profess to believe in the dignity of labor, should make such absurd distinctions. And I am unable to see how the ordinary labor of the farmer, merchant, doctor, or lawyer, can be any more pleasant, interesting, or refining to them, than ordinary housework is to the wife and mother. Is there not as wide a field for the use of brains in her department as in each, or any, of their departments? And is it a small matter—a low ambition—to devote one's time and energies to making a pleasant and attractive home? Do not thousands of men toil uncomplainingly, day after day, all their lives, to give their wives and daughters the means to render home comfortable and attractive? For my part, I can conceive of no nobler aim in life for any woman than that of making a perfect home. Is there any higher or holier object to which she can 'devote all her powers of mind and body'? I know of none. Hence, my desire to aid in establishing this home-school, where girls can be taught to perform thoroughly all life's homely household duties."

"Kate, good men and women everywhere should lend a helping hand to your enterprise," said Emeline, earnestly, after listening attentively to my sermonizing. "The subject assumes a new aspect to me; and I begin to realize that the wives and mothers who allow their daughters to grow up without being educated in all the branches of housekeeping, or who spend their lives in boarding-houses for the purpose of escaping domestic duties, are among the worst foes of society."

"Emeline, your language is forcible, but just," was my reply. "Boarding-houses may be necessary; but they are necessary evils. They destroy all domestic privacy, and are demoralizing society by eating out the heart of our home life. Girls whose training in household duties has been neglected, flee, after marriage, to these places of refuge, to escape the penalty of their bad or neglected training, and the oppression of ignorant, insolent servants; and thus boarding-houses perpetuate the system of which they are the legitimate result,— that wretched system under which women are reared without a knowledge of housework, and are taught to shirk the cares and responsibilities—thereby losing all the joys and comforts —of a home!"

"But this school you speak of," interrupted Emeline, "is not to be solely a training-school for girls in these domestic matters,—is it, Kate?"

"By no means," I answered. "The aim of its projectors is to make it a model school for girls, where they may enter at an early age, and continue as long as they please. I have no expectation that any of our girls will finish their education at school. They will be taught that education is a life-work; that self-development and self-restraint are the primary objects of education; and that, until they have perfectly developed all their faculties, and are capable of restraining their appetites and passions, their education will be incomplete. Instruction will be given in all the branches usually taught in a first-class school for young women, and in many more, as well as in domestic or household economy. In short, Emeline, the object is to establish a home-school worthy of the name, worthy of the nineteenth century, and worthy of the women of America."

"Kate, notwithstanding the slur of the 'Democrat,' you know I've never had any affiliation with 'strong-minded women.' On the contrary, I have been decidedly opposed to most of their movements; but I like this school project of yours. It seems to me a great deal better for women to go to work to correct our social evils in some such practical way, than to go about clamoring for the ballot, and scolding men generally for depriving them of their rights. Have you ever talked with Alice about it? Perhaps it would strike her favorably. And if it should —"

"Why not go into it heart and soul yourself, Cousin Emeline?" I interrupted, eagerly. "Why not put your life and fortune into it? Believe me, it would pay a great deal better than writing novels."

"Pay?" answered Emeline, interrogatively. "I never thought of making money out of my novels."

"No, no, Emeline; you misunderstand me. I think it will pay better than writing novels, in other ways than in money. It will pay in something more enduring than dollars and cents. I think it will pay in —"

"But," interrupted Emeline, "the sun is setting — how beautiful! — and Alice will be wondering what has become of us. Let us go home."

CHAPTER XI.

LITTLE THINGS.

"Cousin Kate, are you going to ignore cake entirely in your cook-book?" asked Alice, one evening at tea, as she passed me the loaf-cake she had made a week before. "Even you sometimes indulge in eating cake."

"Very true, Alice," I replied; "I enjoy this bread-cake, for instance; and quite delight in good ginger-cake at times. But I am so disgusted with the prominence given in cook-books to cake over bread, and I everywhere see so much time and attention bestowed upon cake, and so little upon bread, that I am strongly tempted, in my cook-book, to treat cake of all kinds with silent contempt."

"But," said Emeline, "since people will eat cake, why not tell them how to make a few varieties that are inexpensive and comparatively harmless? This loaf or bread cake is, to my taste, better than the average fruit-cake, for it has a cleaner taste. Yet it doesn't cost quarter as much as the fruit-cake, and is easier made, isn't it, Alice?"

"Yes, mamma, this cake gave me no more trouble to make than would a loaf of bread. From the bread, when perfectly light and ready for the last moulding, I took three cups of dough, to which I added two cups of white sugar, one cup of butter, two eggs well beaten, one cup chopped raisins, one teaspoonful cinnamon, and half a teaspoonful of soda. As the dough was very light I pressed it into the cup, measuring it as full as possible. Placing these ingredients together in an earthen bowl, I worked them with my hand for half an hour. The mixture became quite soft, after being worked awhile. I put it into a well-buttered baking-dish, lined with white paper, and, placing it upon the table covered, let it stand two hours to rise. When light — which was shown by little bubbles of air dotting its surface, more than from its having risen — I placed it in a very moderate oven, not nearly so hot as bread requires, and every few minutes I opened the oven door just enough to peep in and see how it was baking. To my joyful surprise, — for it being my first attempt at bread-cake, I scarcely looked for success, — each time I peeped, I found it rising, rising, rising, slowly, and at last I shut the door, satisfied that I could leave it to bake unwatched. It was in the oven an hour and a half, and you see it came out very nice."

"And how well it keeps," observed Emeline.

"Indeed, I think age improves it, as it does many things."

"And people also," I answered. "Did it ever occur to you, Emeline, how many men and women ripen and mellow — growing sweeter and more tender, as the autumn of life come on? This bread-cake," I continued, "when baked in suitable form, makes a very nice pudding, if steamed, and served hot, with wine or fruit sauce. To my taste it is more palatable than the ordinary plum-pudding, while it is much less indigestible. Bread-cake, doughnuts, and buns —"

"No buns for me," said Emeline. "I detest the whole rusk family. Many people like that half-and-half sort of food — a something between one thing and another — a link joining this thing to that; but my taste is different. If I eat bread, I want it to be bread; if cake, cake; not a combination of both, resulting in neither."

"But mamma," said Alice, "buns are bread etherealized; light, airy things that I delight in eating, because of their very daintiness. My recipe for buns reads in this manner: Whip together three ounces of sugar and three eggs, until well broken and mixed; then pour upon them slowly, continuing the beating meanwhile, a pint of boiling milk. Add a pint of flour, and when lukewarm, a half-gill of yeast. Beat all well together, cover closely, and let stand over night. In the morning add a handful of flour, and beat them soundly. When again light, work well with the hand, adding three ounces of butter and flour very gradually. The excellence of these buns consists mainly in their being soft and elastic or spongy. When the dough is stiff enough to cling together and work away from the sides of the bowl, sufficient flour has been added. Work ten or fifteen minutes longer, cover closely, and leave to rise. When very light, mould into small round cakes, and place in a pan, not allowing the cakes to touch each other. Let them rise in the pan till light; then bake in a moderate oven. Is that right, Cousin Kate?"

"You have omitted flavoring and citron," I said.

"So I have," answered Alice; "I forgot to mention that at the time of adding the butter, lemon or other flavoring may be used according to taste; and that a slice of citron, placed in each bun at the time of forming, gives them a nice flavor, and causes a delightful surprise to the uninitiated eater. By the way, how will this do for doughnuts? Put into a pan three pints of sifted flour. Make a well in the centre, into which put a half pound of sugar, a gill of buttermilk or thick sour milk, two eggs, two ounces of butter, a teaspoonful of soda, and flavoring to taste. With the hand mix these ingredients well together, working in the flour gradually, until the dough is very smooth. It must not, however, be made stiff. Roll upon the moulding-board half an inch thick, cut in form, and fry in boiling lard. When cool, dust the doughnuts with pulverized sugar. Doughnuts made according to this recipe are the nicest I ever ate."

"The next time you make buns, Alice, when the dough is ready to shape, roll it on the moulding-board, cut into doughnuts and fry in boiling lard; and you will, I think, decidedly give them the preference over those made according to your recipe."

"When the flavoring is omitted, and the doughnuts are dusted with pulverized sugar and cinnamon, they suit my taste much better," said Emeline. "And Kate," she added, "a good doughnut isn't a bad thing with a cup of coffee for breakfast."

"A doughnut and a cup of coffee," I answered, "may be well enough for breakfast, sometimes. But, in my opinion, a nice roll, or a slice of good bread, with sweet, rich butter, far outranks doughnuts or cake as an accompaniment of coffee."

"Cousin Kate," said Alice, "my one accomplishment in the culinary art, before I came under your instruction, was the making of delicate cake. I think I was mistress of that. Won't you put my recipe in your book? I use the largest sized stone-china coffee-cup for measure; and to one cup of butter, add three cups of granulated sugar. work to a cream with the hand. Then use a wooden spoon and stir in, a little of each at a time, alternating, one and one-third cups of sweet milk, and four cups of flour in which three teaspoonfuls baking powder have been mixed. Beat well, the more the better. Lastly, add the whites of ten eggs, creamed; that is, beaten to the consistency of cream and not stiffly. Stir in the eggs very carefully, and bake at once."

"In return, Alice, for your nice recipe, which you have so carefully learned, I will add one for sponge cake; for the two ought to go together as being harmonious in delicacy and contrasting prettily in color.

"Weigh ten eggs and take their weight of sugar and half their weight of flour. Reject the yolks of two, and beat whites and yolks separately until perfectly light; then mix and beat together, and by degrees add the sugar and the juice and grated rind of a lemon. Lastly add flour, stirring in carefully. Bake in square pans."

"Alice," said her mother, "while listening to your recipe for delicate cake, I wanted to ask how you measure a third of a cup of milk?"

"I doubt not, mamma, there are better ways of arriving at the solution, but this was mine. I discovered a large iron spoon, and found by measuring, that the cup held just twelve spoonfuls; therefore four gave me the desired one-third."

"Kate, what sort of pickles do you like best, with fried or scalloped oysters?" asked Emeline, turning suddenly from contemplation of sweet things to things sour.

"Cold-slaw," I replied; "cabbage crisp and sweet, with a simple salad dressing. I like it a thousand times better than any pickle that ever was made. Next to eating such quantities of cake and pastry, I think Americans are most absurd in their free use of pickles and condiments. When people can have sliced tomatoes, fresh and delicious, or cool, crisp cabbage, or sour baked apples full of tart spiciness, it is a marvel to me that they should crave mustard, catsup, and pickles. Pickles may be useful, and entitled to a place on our tables in the late winter, or early spring, when fresh vegetables and acid fruits are hard to obtain, and I shall give a few recipes for making them; for it is a pity that housewives should buy, at an exorbitant price, what, with a little trouble, they can make much better for themselves. First among pickles, I shall give chopped cabbage. Select cabbage crisp and sweet; chop it moderately fine; season to taste with white mustard-seed, salt, and pepper. Put it in a jar and cover with cold vinegar. Scatter whole cloves over the top, to prevent mould. Do you know, Emeline, it is said that cloves scattered over any pickle, sweet or sour, will effectually prevent mould? and, so far as I have tested, I have found it to be true. If preferred, sweet peppers may be chopped with the cabbage, instead of using ground pepper."

"It occurs to me, Cousin Kate," said Alice, "this seems a very loose sort of a recipe for you to give who are so particular about weights and measures. You say, 'season to taste.' I think you should designate the amount of salt and pepper."

"Not at all," I replied. "Spicing and flavoring are matters of taste. Some like much, others less; and I think every housewife should use her own discretion, and decide for herself about such matters. Besides, Alice, what I desire above all things is to induce women to think and experiment for themselves in the matter of cooking — to seek out many new ways and inventions, so as to secure improvements upon the old methods. Just as soon as women become convinced that this question of how best to prepare the food we eat, is a momentous one, and that she who excels in answering it deserves high rank among women,— and not only among women, but among public benefactors,— good cooks will abound."

"But when will they become convinced?" asked Emeline, with a sigh.

"Not so long, at least," I answered, "as mothers allow their tables to be furnished with hotly spiced chow-chow and other such abominations, when it is so easy, by taking a little trouble, to substitute this mild tomato sauce: Take twelve ripe tomatoes; peel and slice them. Chop fine, four sweet peppers, ripe or green, and two onions. Place all together in a preserving-kettle, adding two tablespoonfuls of salt, two of sugar, and a pint of vinegar. Simmer two hours, or until quite thick; then bottle for use. Or this green tomato sauce: Take a peck of green tomatoes and ten onions; slice and sprinkle lightly with salt. Let stand over night. In the morning drain the brine or water away from it, and put in a preserving-kettle, with three half gallons of vinegar, three sweet peppers, chopped fine, a quarter of a pound of white mustard-seed, and an ounce of cloves. Boil slowly three or four hours, stirring frequently. Half an hour before removing from the fire add one pound of sugar. Or this cucumber catsup, which is simple and easily made, yet full of pungency: Grate six green cucumbers and three onions. Add to the grated mixture a teaspoonful of salt, and half a teaspoonful of pepper. Drain off the juice, and, after measuring, throw it away, adding to the catsup the same quantity of vinegar. Mix well and bottle for use."

"But," said Emeline, "many people prefer cucumber pickles, pure and simple, to all mixtures, and fancy preparations. Do you know the best method of making them?"

"Perhaps not. But this is a very excellent method: Put the freshly gathered cucumbers in a jar, sprinkle lightly with salt, and when the jar is full of cucumbers pour on as much boiling water as it will hold. After the water becomes cold, remove the cucumbers to a preserving-kettle, cover with weak vinegar, and heat to boiling point. Remove, drain, and put in a jar, distributing among them pieces of sweet pepper. Cover with strong vinegar, in which a few cloves and a small quantity of sugar have been heated. If you wish to improve the color of the pickles, line the kettle, before placing them in it, with green cabbage or grape leaves, and put a small piece of alum in the vinegar."

"But how many cloves and how much sugar do you put in them?" asked Alice.

"An ounce of cloves and a pound of sugar to a gallon of vinegar, is what *I* should use," I replied; "but that is a matter of taste, and, as I said before, I prefer, in such cases not to give weights or measures. I will also add, Alice, that when I speak of vinegar I always mean good, strong cider vinegar, and not the weak, watery, insipid stuff that is often used by housewives, with the almost certain loss of the pickles on which it is used. Yet I notice that people whose pickles spoil from want of good vinegar, generally attribute their having spoiled to some other cause."

"Cousin Kate, I hope you will give some nice methods of sweet pickling, or spicing fruits. Among pickles, sweet or spiced ones are my favorites, although mamma, no doubt, would object to them as occupying neutral ground between pickles and preserves, as being too undecided, not positive enough, in character to suit her."

"Spiced peaches and damsons are both very nice," I answered. "The former I prepare in this manner: Selecting hard free-stone peaches, I cut in halves, and remove the stones before paring, as I find them much easier to remove before than after paring. For seven pounds of fruit I use three pounds of sugar, a quart of vinegar, and a half ounce each of cloves and cinnamon. I put the sugar, with three pints of water, into a preserving-kettle, and when it boils, cook as many of the peaches at a time as the kettle will hold without their being piled one upon another. I cook slowly, turning them over and shaking them about, that they may cook evenly; and when tender, remove by means of a wire skimmer, and place in a jar. When all the fruit is cooked, I simmer the syrup until quite thick, then add vinegar and spice, simmer all together a few minutes, and pour over the peaches.

"Damsons I treat differently. Selecting large, fair plums, I puncture the skins with a fork, and lay them in a stone jar. Then I heat to boiling, four pounds of sugar and a quart of vinegar, with spice, the same as for peaches. When boiling hot I pour the liquor upon the plums, cover closely, and set aside until next morning; then I drain from the plums all the juice, heat to boiling, and pour over them as at first. I repeat this every morning for a week, or until the damsons are soft and tender. I then put all in the kettle together, simmer gently for a few minutes, skim out the fruit and put it in a jar, simmer the syrup twenty or thirty minutes, or until it seems rich and sufficiently thick, then pour it over the fruit, and consider the process of spicing damsons completed. But here comes Tom with our letters and papers."

Our trunks were packed and our arrangements all completed for leaving Maplewood; and as we sat on the piazza in the September twilight after tea, listening to the chirpings of the katydids, Alice observed,—

"Cousin Kate, I would like to linger on here indefinitely. I have never passed a pleasanter summer; and I wish we could stay through October and November, at least, to watch the autumn foliage as it brightens and fades."

"If I had known before making other arrangements," replied Emeline, "that Mrs. Douglas had concluded to remain abroad, I could have been satisfied to stay several months longer; for the summer here has been to me very restful. True, I have not made much progress with my novel; but I think my time has been spent to good advantage. I have looked at life from a different stand-point than ever before, and begin to feel a deep interest in everything that concerns our common humanity. I know I do not realize, as Kate does, its needs and wants; but I accept the fact that no true woman ought to remain idle, or take to novel-writing merely for amusement, or to kill time. The great majority of men and women know so imperfectly how to do the little every-day duties of life, the aggregate of which makes up the sum of human happiness, that they go stumbling and blundering through the world, hoping that somehow, somewhere in the far-off future, they will come up with and enjoy the good time, which through ignorance and laziness they fail to grasp and make for themselves here."

"Ma," interrupted Alice, "you accused me of being unorthodox when I told you that Gerald's musings were such fancies as I frequently indulged in myself, and were not 'wild ravings' as you termed them. It seems to me *you* are stepping off the orthodox platform when you condemn people for hoping and expecting to have a good time prepared for them by some unseen power hereafter, when they are too stupid or lazy to make it for themselves here, where they have the materials for so doing lying all about them."

"Alice," I interposed, "you and your mother seem to me to differ about non-essentials only. You both admit that your views of life have changed within the past few months; and you both agree that an idle, selfish, aimless life is the lowest possible form of human existence. It is very evident, therefore, that you have both changed positions: and if orthodoxy means remaining stationary, — always of the same belief, — it must be conceded that both of you are less orthodox than you were a few months ago. People who use their eyes and brains learn to see and do things differently, and of course to think differently about them, nearly every day. And until they do use these organs, it is folly to expect much progress or improvement to be made in the world. The great majority of people, as you say, do not know how to do the little every-day duties of life that lie all about them. Why do they not? Is it from ignorance, stupidity, or laziness? It seems scarcely credible that men and women with ordinary sense can go through the world without noticing the thousands of little things that are component parts of their every-day life. It is hard to believe that a girl could grow up in a house where three meals are prepared every day, and when she arrives at womanhood have no knowledge of how to prepare a breakfast, dinner, or supper. Yet I presume each of us is personally acquainted with fifty young women who do not know how to broil a beefsteak, or bake a potato; and haven't the faintest idea of the first principles of bread-making. It is a burning shame to our sex that so many of us are content to grow up thus ignorant, and no wonder women have not obtained the ballot. But while men sneer at us, and with justice too, for such shiftlessness and inefficiency, they are, in respect to using their eyes and brains, not one whit better than women. I know scores of great, hulking fellows who have warmed themselves by coal fires all their lives, and yet can't kindle a coal fire in a grate or stove; or can't, when it is kindled, keep it burning two consecutive days. It is the rule, and not the exception, to forget and neglect life's every-day duties. The world suffers more from heedlessness than from criminality; and we wrong ourselves and others as much by want of thought as by want of heart. We are continually worrying and annoying ourselves and all who are intimately associated with us by neglecting, or forgetting to do, our every-day duties. Our eyes and brains were given us for a beneficent purpose; but most of us fail to discover their use, or to use them to much practical advantage. A great portion of life is wasted, and much vital force consumed, in correcting the evil results of ignorance, negligence, and forgetfulness; or in doing labor that could be avoided by a moderate use of common-sense. Why should any housewife suffer her fires to go out every few days in midwinter through carelessness, and thus endanger the health of some member of the family, as well as waste the time of some one in rebuilding them? Or, why should she induce dyspepsia, discomfort, and general disgust in the household, by making bad bread, bad butter, or bad food of any kind, when she could have the best of everything by a little care and attention? Or why should men and women who have homes, permit things in and about them to get out of order and remain so for weeks and months, to the almost hourly annoyance and discomfort of every one in the family? Go among the homes all over our land, and in a majority of them you will find the occupants suffering discomfort and inconvenience from a dozen trifling things that they do not seem to observe, or are too stupid and inefficient to remedy. For instance, a door sags on account of a loose screw in one of its hinges, and causes extra labor every time it is opened or closed; or, its hinges squeak for need of a few drops of oil, and disturb every one in the house a dozen times a day; or a window-shutter bangs and flaps for want of a fastening, till it eventually tumbles off and is broken; or a pump gets out of order, and, for want of a slight repair, has to be labored with every time a bucket of water is needed. And so I could go on and on, and mention a thousand similar things that any one of thought and observation can see almost daily, and on every one of which extra labor and strength are wasted, week after week, and month after month, when a few moments' thoughtful, intelligent effort would put any one of them in perfect condition. Yet people endure such extra labor and discomfort without seeming to realize that they can avoid them by removing the cause. Through all the various departments of society, the disposition to forget, neglect, overlook, or remain ignorant how to do minor things, as they are termed, is so apparent that it is rather difficult to get a correct idea of what the average man and woman conceive to be the chief end of existence. I am old-fashioned enough to think that people who endeavor to escape the so-called drudgeries of life, by shirking and neglecting its ever-present duties and responsibilities, soon become incapable of appreciating and enjoying its purest delights and satisfactions, and fritter away their time, vainly searching for a sphere in which they can labor to the best advantage; or spend it, avariciously striving to get up 'a corner' on the fruits of the future, and monopolize the whole stock of happiness supposed to be garnered up in the storehouse of the 'good time coming.'"

"Kate, it seems to me you are right, in the main," said Emeline. "But you wouldn't have people give too much time to little things, would you?"

"Too much time! Why, Emeline, the more I think upon this subject, the more I am impressed with its magnitude and importance. What do people mean when they talk of being so engrossed with great things that they forget, or neglect, little ones? Great and small are but relative terms; and great things are simply the aggregate of many small ones. Who can determine where the dividing line between big and little should be drawn; or exactly how many little things are required in the composition of one big thing? Is the size of things, their importance or unimportance, their bigness or littleness, accurately computed by the amount of time, labor, care, strength, or intellect bestowed upon them; or by the effect they produce upon the world? Or is it carelessly measured by an imaginary standard for whose correctness no one is responsible? Are the great things of life those that give society at large the greatest amount of happiness; or those that yield a few persons the greatest amount of money? Does the surgeon who performs a dangerous operation on a patient do a great thing, and the nurse who faithfully watches and ministers to that patient do a small thing? Does the preacher who delivers a learned doctrinal discourse do a great thing, and the layman who, by a few kind words, encourages some weak or wayward brother or sister to live a purer and better life, do a little thing? Does the lawyer who, for a heavy fee, defends and acquits a criminal, do a great thing, and the 'peace-maker,' who, without pay, protects the property, or saves the life of a neighbor, do a little thing? Does the stock-jobber who amasses a million in a month by obtaining control of a corporation, and by watering or skilfully manipulating its stock, do a big thing, and the mechanic who toils faithfully a lifetime, and earns only his daily bread, do a little thing? Does the speculator who buys up the products of a thousand farms or workshops, and, by thus controlling the market, makes a fortune in a week, do a big thing; while the owners of those farms and workshops, who toiled diligently for months, and obtained but small gains, did little things? Does the man of wealth who buys a tract of land for a few thousand dollars, and holds it unimproved till it increases in value to millions, do a big thing; and do the thousands of men of humble means, who buy of him at the increased price, and improve and beautify their purchases with pleasant homes, do little things? Who shall say that the woman who remains quietly at home, doing daily, and with systematic neatness, the housewifely duties that render all within her influence contented and happy, is not teaching her sister women as wisely, and doing as much for the world's moral, social, and political advancement, as the one who travels from the Atlantic to the Pacific, eloquently pleading the right of her sex to larger liberty or wider privileges? Or, which one of us is able to decide that a little poem, wrought out in obscurity, and for which its author received a few dollars only, has not effected a greater good in the world than the gigantic enterprise, inaugurated with ostentatious display and applause, that has put millions in the pocket of its projector?

"If, then, we accept the principle that it is the duty of every man and woman to be engaged in work that is useful in some way to the world, why is it not as well to make beds, sweep rooms, and cook dinners, as it is to plough fields, build houses, and buy and sell corn and cotton? And when a woman's duty lies in the way of the former, rather than of the latter occupations, why should it be distasteful to her to acquaint herself with all the details of housekeeping? Or, why should she consider it drudgery to spend her time in doing, in the most perfect manner, those little household economies that add so much to the comfort and happiness of life?

"To teach their children self-restraint, — the control of their appetites and passions, — should be a paramount consideration with all parents; for people who simply live to eat, or, as the poet puts it, —

> 'who creep
> Into the world to eat and sleep,
> And know no reason why they're born
> But merely to consume the corn,
> Devour the cattle, fowl, and fish,
> And leave behind an empty dish,' —

are vagabonds and drones, who steal and consume the substance of those who labor and produce. Nevertheless, we must all eat to live; and the food we eat should be prepared in the best manner. Men and women are the most perfect creations of the Maker of the universe, and are designed for the performance of labor of the highest order; but unless the conditions of their existence are complied with, and the materials that are required to keep them in working order are prepared with skilfulness and care, it is impossible for them to do the best work and lead the truest lives.

"The sum of the whole matter, then, is this: That the great things of life are composed of, and dependent on, its little things; and the more care and attention that are bestowed upon necessary little things, the more successful will be the endeavor, and the greater the result, of all human effort."

"Cousin Kate," said Alice, "as you commenced your discourse without a text, you might appropriately terminate it with one. For instance,

> 'Little drops of water,
> Little grains of sand,
> Make the mighty ocean
> And the pleasant land.'

And since you appear to be able to preach almost as well as you can cook, you might, in case you relinquish your idea of publishing a cook-book, favor the world with a volume of sermons. But, jesting aside, I think I have learned more this summer than ever before in the same length of time; and I am sure I have been more contented and happy."

"Alice, you express my sentiments, also," said Emeline. "Therefore, if my novel should remain forever unfinished, and Cousin Kate's cook-book never be written — even should our expectations fail to be realized in the Home-School — still the lives of us three will be richer and sweeter, for having spent our summer at Maplewood, although much of our time has been spent in COOKING AND CASTLE-BUILDING."

INDEX.

	Page
Yeast,	16
Bread,	19
Graham bread,	31
Rolls,	32
Egg rolls,	34
Cream biscuit,	38
Strawberry shortcake,	40
Maryland biscuit,	41
Picked-up codfish,	44
Oatmeal mush,	44
Baked potatoes,	44
To boil milk,	47
Fried chicken,	50
Fried fish,	51
Graham gems,	52
Fine flour gems,	52
Graham cakes,	52
Hasty pudding,	54
Cracked wheat,	54
Hominy grits,	55
Stewed chicken,	56
Stewed chicken with mushrooms,	57
Stewed beef,	57
Stewed veal,	57
Bread cakes,	70
Rice cakes,	71
Waffles,	71
Waffles, No. 2,	72
Waffles, No. 3,	72
Flannel cakes,	73
Muffins,	73
Buckwheat cakes,	74
Buckwheat cakes, No. 2,	75
Corn dodgers,	77
Corn muffins,	78
Corn griddle-cakes,	79
Corn slappers,	79
Cape May bread,	80
Coffee,	83
Black tea,	91
Green tea,	92
Toast,	93
Green pease,	95
Asparagus,	96
String beans,	96
Lima beans,	96
Stewed beans,	97
Baked beans,	97
Boston baked beans,	97
Stewed corn,	99
Corn oysters,	99
Boiled potatoes,	100
Mashed potatoes,	101
Fried potatoes,	102
Stewed potatoes,	102
Browned potatoes,	102
Soup,	104
Broth,	107
Roast lamb,	107
Roast veal,	108
Roast beef,	108
Boiled meats,	109
Boiled fowls,	109

INDEX.

	Page		Page
Boiled ham,	109	Apple sauce,	154
Boiled onions,	111	Tapioca pudding,	155
Boiled beets,	111	Tapioca pudding, No. 2,	155
Boiled cabbage,	111	Serving berries,	157
Boiled turnips,	111	Egg plant,	165
Boiled dandelion,	111	Fried tomatoes,	167
Boiled spinach,	111	Fried oysters,	168
Beef and tomato sauce,	111	Scalloped oysters,	170
Rice pudding,	113	Fish-balls,	172
Boiled rice,	116	Fresh-fish balls,	173
Boiled rice, No. 2,	116	Hash,	173
Broiled steak,	123	Hashed-meat cakes,	174
Broiled chops,	124	Scrapple,	174
Fried mutton chops,	124	Hashed potato,	175
Broiled lamb chops,	125	Chicken croquettes,	175
Broiled chicken,	126	Tomato stew,	176
Broiled quail,	127	Loaf cake,	190
Roast wild duck,	128	Steamed fruit pudding,	192
Stewed terrapin,	129	Buns,	192
Omelet,	130	Doughnuts,	193
Salad dressing,	135	Raised doughnuts,	194
Chicken salad,	136	Delicate cake,	194
Salad dressing, No. 2,	136	Sponge cake,	195
Frizzled beef,	137	Cold slaw,	196
Berry mush,	144	Pickled cabbage,	196
Currant jam,	144	Mild tomato sauce,	198
Currant jelly,	145	Green tomato pickle,	198
Pastry,	149	Cucumber catsup,	198
Apple pie,	149	Cucumber pickle,	199
Linen pie,	151	Spiced peaches,	200
Baked apples,	153	Spiced damsons,	201
Baked apples, No. 2,	154		

CLASSIFIED INDEX.

BREAKFAST DISHES.

	Page		Page
Beef, frizzled,	137	Fish, fried,	51
Cakes, bread,	70	Gems, Graham,	52
" buckwheat,	74	" fine flour,	52
" " No. 2,	75	Grits, hominy,	55
" corn,	76	Hash,	173
" flannel,	73	Hasty pudding,	54
" hashed meat,	174	Mush, oatmeal,	44
" rice,	71	Omelet with parsley,	131
Chicken, broiled,	126	Oysters, corn,	99
" fried,	50	Potatoes, baked,	44
" croquettes,	175	" fried,	102
Chops, broiled lamb,	125	" hashed,	175
" " mutton,	125	" stewed,	102
" fried "	124	Scrapple,	174
Cracked wheat,	54	Slappers, corn,	79
Dodgers, corn,	77	Stew, tomato,	176
Egg-plant, fried,	165	Waffles,	71
Fish-balls,	172	" No. 2,	72
" of fresh fish,	173	" No. 3,	72

DINNER DISHES.

	Page		Page
Asparagus,	96	Cabbage, boiled,	111
Beans, baked,	97	Chicken, plain stewed,	56
" Boston baked,	97	" stewed with mushrooms,	57
" lima,	96	Dandelions, boiled,	111
" stewed,	97	Duck, wild, roasted,	128
" string,	96	Fowls, boiled,	109
Beef, boiled with tomato sauce,	111	Ham, boiled,	109
" roasted,	108	Lamb, roasted,	107
" stewed,	57	Onions,	111
Broth,	107	Oysters, scalloped,	170

[215]

CLASSIFIED INDEX.

	Page		Page
Pease, green,	95	Spinach,	111
Potatoes, boiled,	100	Terrapin, stewed,	129
" browned,	102	Tomatoes, fried,	167
" mashed,	101	Turnips, boiled,	111
Rice,	116	Veal, roasted,	103
" No. 2,	116	" stewed,	57
Soup,	104		

RELISHES AND PICKLES.

	Page		Page
Cabbage, pickled,	196	Peaches, spiced,	200
Catsup, cucumber,	198	Salad dressing,	135
Cold slaw,	196	" " No. 2,	136
Damsons, spiced,	201	Tomatoes, pickled green,	198
Mild tomato sauce,	198		

DESSERTS.

	Page		Page
Coffee,	86	Pudding, steamed fruit,	192
" No. 2,	88	" tapioca,	155
Mush, fruit,	144	" " No. 2,	155
Pastry,	149	Shortcake, strawberry,	40
Pies,	146	Tea, black,	91
Pie, apple,	149	" green,	92
Pudding, rice,	113		

TEA DISHES.

	Page		Page
Apples,	141	Doughnuts, No. 2,	194
Berries,	143	Jam, currant,	144
" serving,	157	Jelly, "	145
Biscuit, cream,	38	Muffins, corn,	78
" Maryland,	41	" wheat,	73
Bread, Cape May corn,	80	Oysters, fried,	168
Buns,	192	Quail, broiled,	127
Cake, delicate,	194	Rolls, plain,	32
" loaf,	190	" with egg,	34
" sponge,	195	Salad, chicken,	136
Doughnuts,	193	Toast,	93

www.ingramcontent.com/pod-product-compliance
Lightning Source LLC
Chambersburg PA
CBHW020815230426
43666CB00007B/1022